SPACE

THE OFFICIAL PLANETARIUM BOOK

SPACE

THE OFFICIAL PLANETARIUM BOOK

Sue Becklake

Prima Publishing
3875 Atherton Road
Rocklin, CA 95765
(916) 632 4400

PRIMA

Prima Publishing, Rocklin, CA 95765

Printed and bound in Italy

96 95 94 93 10 9 8 7 6 5 4 3 2 1

ISBN 1-55958-583-8

CONTENTS

A shuttle orbiting
in space.

FOREWORD

This year, 1994, marks the 25th anniversary of the first human walk on the Moon. This historic occasion, which took place on July 20th, 1969, marked a turning point in our exploration of space. In Neil Armstrong's now legendary phrase, it was "...one small step for a man and one giant leap for mankind". Since then our knowledge of space has increased enormously, with such missions as Voyager spacecraft sent to explore the outer planets and the Hubble Space Telescope which has provided many new and fascinating images of outer space.

We are now beginning a new and great chapter in the history of space exploration. We are starting, slowly, to combine the strengths of the two greatest spacefaring nations in the world — the United States and Russia. We are going to stop preparing to destroy each other in war and work together to deliver enormous benefits to people everywhere.

We have already taken the first few steps. A Russian cosmonaut flew aboard a NASA Space Shuttle in February 1994. Two U.S. astronauts are in Russia training for one of them to fly on the Russian Mir space station in early 1995. The next step after that will probably be the most difficult and significant thing we have done since the Moon landing. A Space Shuttle will

A Saturn rocket launches the Apollo astronauts.

dock with the Mir to perform scientific research and carry the U.S. astronauts back to Earth.

The knowledge that we gain from the Mir mission and future joint missions will prepare us for the next giant step, an international space station that will begin to take shape in orbit in 1997. This will be the biggest peacetime technological venture in history.

Once the nations of the world have learned how to live and work together in space on a regular basis and the world economy improves, we should be ready for the ultimate adventure: sending humans to Mars. Now, more than ever before, it is time to look toward the heavens and soar like eagles, reaching out for knowledge and inspiration in the far reaches of the universe.

Daniel S. Goldin,
NASA Administrator

An astronaut's footprint on the surface of the Moon.

1

ORIGINS OF ASTRONOMY

From earliest times people have been fascinated by the patterns made by the brilliant stars they saw in the sky. Early astronomers tried to explain the movements of the Sun, Moon, stars and planets, but they could not see very far into space. Now astronomers have huge telescopes and satellites in space to help them unravel the mysteries of the Universe.

While this picture was being taken, the stars made trails in the sky. This happens because the Earth is always spinning around.

GODS IN THE SKY

Astronomy is often called the oldest science. It is easy to see why, if you have ever looked at the sky on a very clear, dark night, in a place where there are no city lights. It is an amazing sight consisting of thousands of stars, some much brighter than others, and the pale strip of the Milky Way across the middle.

Before we had artificial streetlights, people were much more familiar with the night sky. They watched the Moon change its shape from a thin crescent to a full circle and back again every few weeks. In ancient times people thought that the Sun, Moon, and stars were gods.

The patterns made by the stars do not change. Thousands of years ago people in places like China, Egypt, and Mesopotamia (modern-day Iraq) imagined the stars made pictures in the sky. They named the star groups for animals or their gods or the heroes of their stories. We still use some of their names today for these star patterns, or "constellations" — they are all listed in the back of this book in the Data Pages.

Some of the sights in the sky were very frightening to people who did not understand them. Sometimes a bright new star with a long shining tail appeared from nowhere. We know that this "hairy" star was a comet, but in those days people thought it was a warning of disaster.

Equally terrifying was when the Sun disappeared in the middle of the day. The Chinese thought a dragon had gobbled up the Sun. Really it was an eclipse, just the Moon blocking out the Sun's light. Astronomers of the day realized that eclipses happened regularly so they could predict when the next would occur. However, this was a dangerous job — an astronomer might be executed if he made a mistake and an eclipse happened unexpectedly.

TELLING THE TIME

Early astronomers used the constant movement of the Sun, Moon, and stars across the sky to measure time. A day is just the time between one sunrise and the next, but other measurements are not so obvious. The first calendars were based upon the changing shape of the Moon — in fact, the word "month" comes from "Moon." It takes about 29.5 days from one full Moon to the next.

The star patterns move across the sky every night but they also change with the seasons — we see different constellations in the summer and winter. These changes indicated to the farmers when spring was coming and their crops should be sown. In Egypt, the appearance of the bright star Sirius in the morning sky, just before the rising of the Sun, occurred each year at the same time as the River Nile was about to flood, making the dry desert soil fertile for the farmers' crops.

Ancient Arab astronomers made very careful measurements of the planets as they moved across the sky. Many bright stars still have Arab names.

A STONE CALENDAR

About 3,500 years ago a circle of huge stones, called Stonehenge, was built in Britain. It is possible that it was used as a giant calendar to observe the positions of the Sun. The stones were carefully lined up in accordance with the rising and setting of the Sun and Moon at particular times of the year. Modern calendars are based on a year, which is the time it takes the Earth to circle round the Sun — that is, 365.25 days. Because of this extra quarter day, every four years we have a Leap Year of 366 days.

GREEK ASTRONOMER-SCIENTISTS

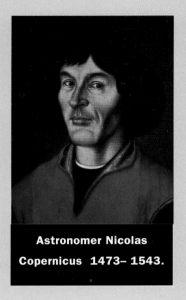

Astronomer Nicolas Copernicus 1473– 1543.

About 5,000 years ago scientists tried to explain what they saw in the sky. They understood why eclipses happened and why the Moon seemed to change its shape, but they also wanted to explain the movements of the Sun, the Moon, and the five "wandering stars." These wanderers were named Mercury, Venus, Mars, Jupiter, and Saturn after the gods of Roman mythology.

They are of course the five planets that we can see easily in the sky without a telescope. They looked like bright stars but the Greeks could see that they moved across the patterns made by the fixed stars in the sky.

Although the Earth seems flat to anyone living on it, the Greeks realized that it is shaped like a huge round ball. They imagined that the Earth was at the middle of an enormous hollow sphere, with the stars fixed to the inside of it. The sphere rotated around the Earth once every 24 hours so that it made one complete turn each day. They thought that the Sun, Moon, and planets went around the Earth in perfect circles, inside the celestial sphere. All this was described by Ptolemy, a Greek astronomer who lived about 1,850 years ago. Although it was not correct, it was believed for over 1,000 years.

circled around the central Sun. The Moon circled around the Earth which was just another planet, no longer at the middle of everything. Although this was basically correct, Copernicus still wrongly believed that the planets moved in perfect circles.

Later in the 16th century, another great astronomer, Tycho Brahe, made very accurate measurements of the positions of the stars and planets using instruments he built at his observatory in Denmark. He did not believe Copernicus' ideas, but his work helped to prove them. His assistant,

REVOLUTION IN ASTRONOMY

The first real challenge to the idea of the planets circling the Earth came from a Polish monk named Copernicus. Like other astronomers at the time, he realized that Ptolemy's explanation did not fit the actual movements of the planets very well.

In 1543, he published a book describing his idea that the Earth and the other five known planets

Old star map showing the stars of the northern sky.

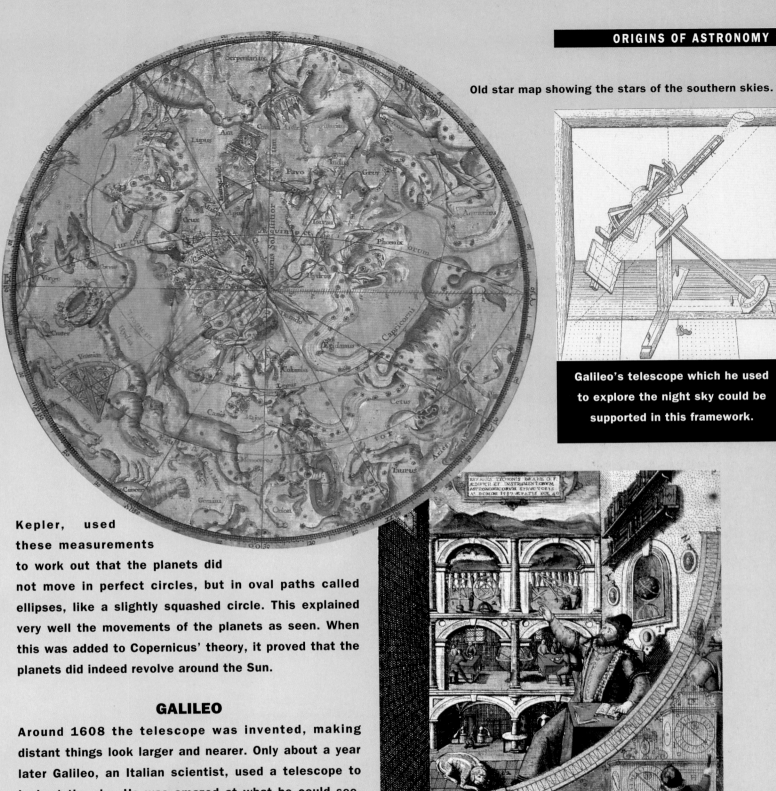

Old star map showing the stars of the southern skies.

Galileo's telescope which he used to explore the night sky could be supported in this framework.

Kepler, used these measurements to work out that the planets did not move in perfect circles, but in oval paths called ellipses, like a slightly squashed circle. This explained very well the movements of the planets as seen. When this was added to Copernicus' theory, it proved that the planets did indeed revolve around the Sun.

GALILEO

Around 1608 the telescope was invented, making distant things look larger and nearer. Only about a year later Galileo, an Italian scientist, used a telescope to look at the sky. He was amazed at what he could see. There were craters on the Moon and large dark areas that he thought might be seas. He discovered Jupiter's four largest moons and saw that they circled around the planet. For the first time it was possible to see that the Milky Way was made up of countless numbers of stars. Galileo could also see many more faint stars through his telescope than he could with his eyes alone.

Tycho Brahe (in the middle of this picture) used huge instruments, like this measuring circle, to plot the movements of the stars and planets accurately.

13

NEWTON

In about 1687 an English scientist, Isaac Newton, discovered the force of gravity, which pulls things toward each other. The Earth's gravity pulls us all down to the ground and stops us from floating away. It also keeps the Moon circling in its orbit around the Earth. The Sun's gravity holds the Earth and planets in their orbits. Gravity is the force that holds the Universe together.

Newton also invented a different kind of telescope. It used a curved mirror, instead of a lens, to collect the starlight and produced clearer images than the earlier telescopes. Most large modern telescopes are based on Newton's design. They are called "reflecting" telescopes.

DISCOVERIES WITH THE TELESCOPE

William Herschel took up astronomy as a hobby. He built his own reflecting telescopes and with one of these he discovered a new planet called Uranus in 1781. It was the first new planet to be discovered — all the other planets out as far as Saturn had been familiar to astronomers for thousands of years.

This discovery made Herschel famous, but he also looked beyond the planets to study the distant stars. He counted the numbers of stars he could see in different parts of the sky, and discovered that the Sun is part of a huge family of stars called the Galaxy. He also suggested that there might be other galaxies outside ours. His sister, Caroline, worked very closely with him and discovered many comets.

Astronomers continue to build bigger and better telescopes and make many more discoveries. They have

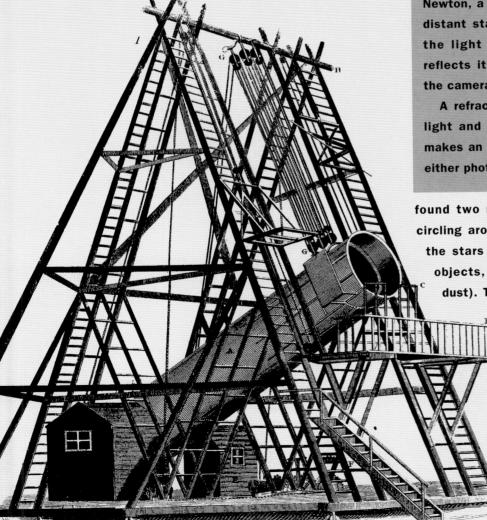

REFLECTING AND REFRACTING TELESCOPES

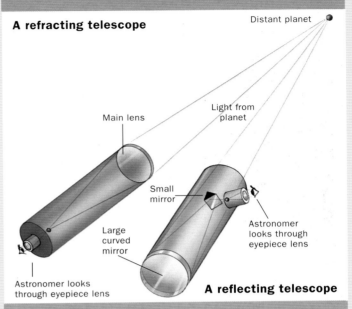

A refracting telescope

Distant planet

Main lens

Light from planet

Small mirror

Large curved mirror

Astronomer looks through eyepiece lens

Astronomer looks through eyepiece lens

A reflecting telescope

In a reflecting telescope, like the one designed by Newton, a large curved mirror collects the light from distant stars or planets. This large mirror reflects the light and focuses it, then a smaller mirror reflects it onto the astronomer's eyepiece or into the camera to be photographed.

A refracting telescope uses a lens to collect the light and focus it to a point. A second lens then makes an image (picture) which the astronomer can either photograph or look at.

found two more planets beyond Uranus, and moons circling around many of the planets. They have listed the stars and their positions, and discovered other objects, for example, nebulae (clouds of gas and dust). They have tried to measure the distances to the stars and to discover what the stars are made of. Finding out about the Universe is never-ending, and exciting discoveries continue.

Herschel's largest telescope had a mirror 49 inches (124 cm) across and was the largest telescope known at the time. Today, modern telescopes are housed in huge domes (far left).

MODERN TELESCOPES

Modern astronomers use huge telescopes to explore the sky. These telescopes tend to be grouped together in observatories built high on mountain-tops. They must be as high as possible, where the air is thinner, because the Earth's atmosphere can spoil astronomical photographs. Even when the sky seems to be clear, just the movements of the air can blur the pictures. Observatories must also be as far as possible from cities. This is because the faint starlight is easily swamped when the sky is lit up by the bright lights of the city.

Most modern telescopes are reflecting telescopes with large mirrors. The larger the collecting mirror, the more light it can collect and the fainter the stars it can see. The biggest reflecting telescope is in Russia and has a mirror 19 feet 8 inches (6m) across.

Today astronomers do not sit and look through their telescopes, drawing what they see, like Galileo and the Herschels did. Instead of their eyes they use cameras. These are able to collect light over a long period, sometimes all night. The very faint light adds up during this time, producing detailed pictures of very distant objects. Computers are often used to add false colors to these pictures which will show up small differences in brightness or temperature.

The Earth is always spinning around and this, of course, is why the stars gradually move across the sky during the night. If a telescope stayed pointing in the same direction while an astronomical photograph was being taken, the picture would therefore be blurred. To stop this from happening, telescopes are driven by motors so that they can track the stars as the Earth moves.

Large modern telescopes need accurate mirrors. Some use several smaller mirrors in one telescope. For example, in Arizona, the Multiple Mirror Telescope has six smaller mirrors, each of them 6 feet (1.8m) across. Together these act like one big mirror 14 feet 9 inches (4.5m) in diameter.

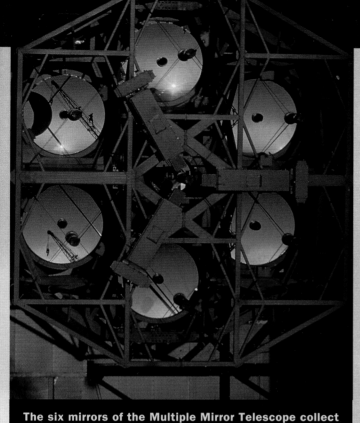

The six mirrors of the Multiple Mirror Telescope collect the faint light from distant stars and galaxies.

RADIO ASTRONOMY

We see the stars because our eyes can detect the light that comes from them. However, stars, galaxies and huge clouds of dust and gas in space also give out other kinds of radiation, similar to light but invisible to our eyes. This radiation includes x-rays, ultraviolet light, infrared radiation and radio waves.

Fortunately, the atmosphere around the Earth acts like a shield, stopping much of the dangerous radiation from reaching the ground. Fortunately, that is, except for those astronomers who would like to study it. This radiation carries information about some of the most interesting and mysterious objects out in space.

The Earth's atmosphere lets most radio waves through to ground level. Astronomers collect these with radio telescopes, which often look like huge saucer-shaped dishes. The dish collects the radio waves just like the mirror in an ordinary telescope. To get more detailed radio pictures, several dishes can be linked together to act like one giant telescope.

The Very Large Array in New Mexico has 27 dishes each approximately 82 feet (25m) across, arranged in a Y-shape with arms about 12.5 miles (20km) long.

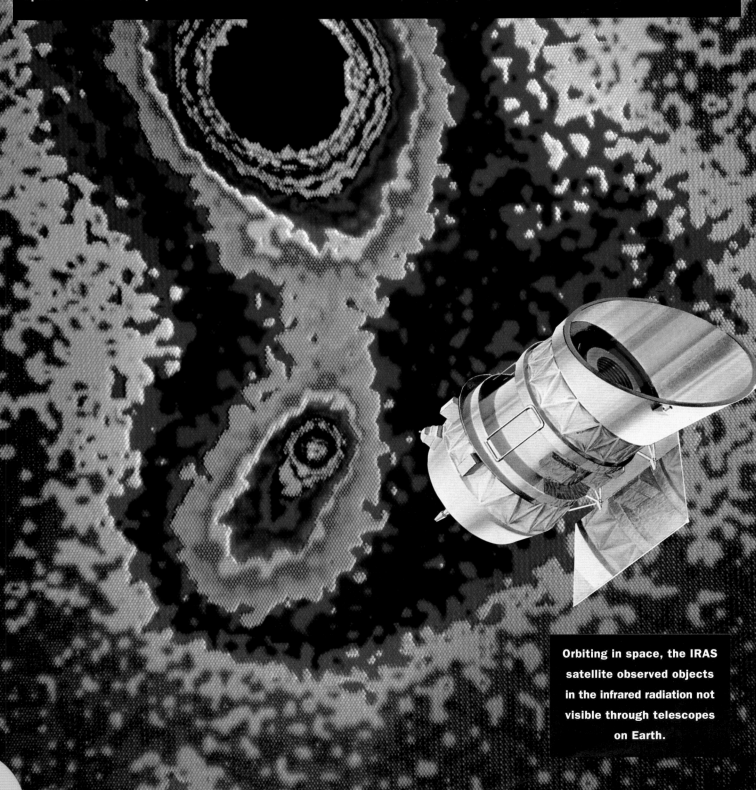

SPACE AGE ASTRONOMY

For the past 30 years astronomers have been able to study many different kinds of radiation. They have put telescopes on satellites which circle around the Earth in space. These send pictures and information back down to the astronomers on Earth. X-ray telescopes can pick up the x-rays from very hot gases. Infrared telescopes "see" the heat from the warm clouds surrounding new stars. Satellites have given astronomers a fascinating, but often puzzling, new view of the Universe.

Orbiting in space, the IRAS satellite observed objects in the infrared radiation not visible through telescopes on Earth.

THE HUBBLE SPACE TELESCOPE

The Hubble Space Telescope was launched in 1990. It is just like an ordinary telescope but it orbits above the Earth's atmosphere. Without the moving air to blur the pictures, its instruments should have been able to see much more distant objects than even the largest telescope on Earth. Unfortunately, its pictures were not as clear as expected because of a fault with the telescope mirrors. Instead of a star looking like a point of light, it appeared as a fuzzy circle. Computers were able to improve the pictures, but could not overcome the problem entirely.

In 1993, while the telescope was still in space, the Space Shuttle astronauts fitted extra mirrors to make it as good as new. Now it can see details, and even individual stars, in galaxies 10 times further away than before. Astronomers hope that its discoveries from the far corners of the Universe will help them to understand how the Universe began.

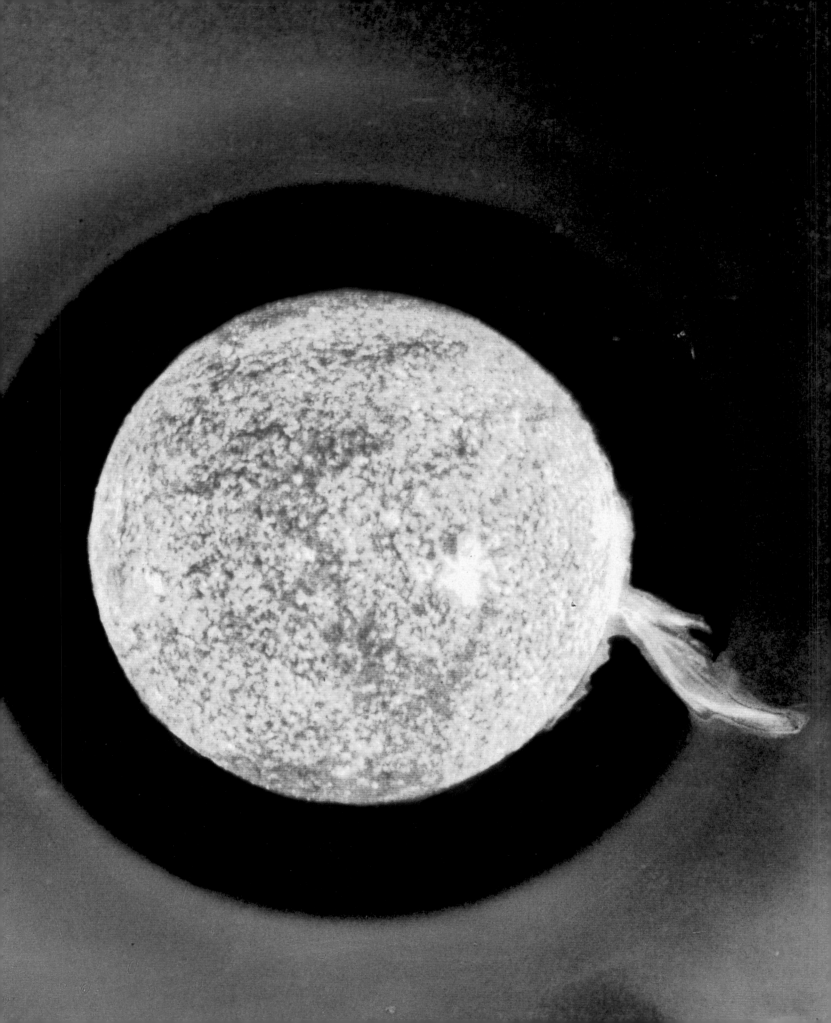

OUR SOLAR SYSTEM

The Earth and all the planets are part of a family that we call the Solar System. This family belongs to the Sun which is right at its center — the planets all circle around the Sun. There are nine planets: Mercury, Venus, Earth, Mars, Jupiter, Saturn, Uranus, Neptune, and Pluto. All but two of them are accompanied by their own systems of circling moons. There are over 60 moons altogether in the Solar System. The family also includes many smaller members. There are the asteroids, which are groups of thousands of tiny planets, and countless numbers of comets. The Solar System is held together by the pull of the Sun's gravity. The planets, moons, and asteroids all shine by reflecting the Sun's light.

A tongue of hot gas, termed a prominence, leaps up from the Sun.

HOW BIG IS THE SOLAR SYSTEM?

Although the Solar System does not have a definite edge its diameter is usually measured across the orbit of the outermost planet, Pluto. This is almost 7,500 million miles (12,000 million km) across, or about 80 times the distance between the Earth and the Sun.

There are vast distances between everything in the Solar System. For instance, the Earth is about 93 million miles (150 million km) from the Sun. The jet airliner Concorde would take over eight years to travel that distance at its normal cruising speed of 1,243 miles per hour (2,000 km per hour).

Astronomers have special ways of measuring these vast distances. They use the distance between the Earth and the Sun as a basic unit of measurement called an astronomical unit (AU). Other distances are compared to this; for instance the outermost planet, Pluto, is over 39 AU away from the Sun (39 times further away than the Earth is), while the innermost planet, Mercury, orbits at less than one-third AU (one-third of the distance between the Earth and the Sun).

The distances between the stars are even more enormous and astronomers use even larger units of distance to measure them. One of these is a light year, which is the distance that light travels in one year — about 5.9 million million miles (9.5 million million km). The nearest star to the Sun is more than four light years away. Light from the Sun takes about eight minutes to reach the Earth so we say that the Earth is eight light minutes from the Sun. Pluto, at a distance of 3,666 million miles (5,900 million km), is 5.5 light hours from the Sun.

To give you some idea of the emptiness of the Solar System, imagine that the Sun is the size of a grapefruit, about 4 1/4 inches (110mm) across. At this scale, the Earth would be the size of a pinhead and would be about 39 feet (12m) — just over the width of a tennis court away from the Sun. The largest planet, Jupiter, would be about as big as a small marble, nearly half an inch (10mm) across, and about 200 feet (60m) away. Distant Pluto would be no larger than the dot at the end of this sentence and would be about 1,500 feet (460m) — the length of five football fields away.

WHIRLING THROUGH SPACE

On Earth we see the Sun, Moon and planets moving slowly across the sky. But this is very misleading because in fact they are all moving through space incredibly fast. The Earth is traveling around the Sun at a speed of 66,662 miles (107,280km) an hour, over 50 times faster than Concorde! All the other planets are traveling around the Sun as well. The speediest is Mercury, the nearest planet to the Sun. It travels at 107,130 miles (172,404km) an hour. Pluto is the slowest at 10,600 miles (17,064km) per hour, less than a tenth of Mercury's speed.

The planets also spin round as they travel through space. The Earth takes 24 hours to complete a turn on its axis. This means that it is rotating at a dizzying 1,038 miles

Compare the different sizes of the Sun, Mercury, Venus, Earth, Mars, Jupiter, Saturn, Uranus, Neptune, and Pluto.

These circles show how the nine planets move around the Sun. You can also see a comet with a tail traveling around the Sun in a long, thin orbit.

(1,670km) an hour. The fastest spinner is the planet Jupiter, taking only 9 hours 50 minutes to spin once. Its cloudy surface is traveling round at about 28,000 miles (45,000km) an hour.

ORBITS

The path of anything moving in space is called its orbit. The planets, asteroids, and comets orbit around the Sun, while moons orbit around their parent planets. These orbits are termed ellipses; they look a little like squashed circles, and can be almost round or very long and thin. Most planets have orbits that are nearly circular, while comets have very long, thin orbits often stretching from beyond Pluto at one extreme to come very close to the Sun at the other.

Most of these orbits can be imagined as lying in a thin disk stretching out around the center of the Sun. The planets all move in the same direction around the Sun — in the opposite direction to the hands of a clock, if you imagine you are looking down from above the Sun's north pole. Most planets and moons also spin in this direction.

THE BIRTH OF THE SOLAR SYSTEM

The planets grew from a disk of gas and dust that swirled around the new young Sun.

Scientists believe that the Solar System began life as a cloud of dust and gas. Gravity pulled the cloud inward and toward the middle, making it smaller but more dense (thicker). As it shrank, the cloud heated up in the center and the Sun started to form.

Some of the left-over cloud flattened out into a disk shape spinning around the new Sun. Gas and dust particles in this disk bumped into each other, sticking together and making larger lumps. These gradually grew into planets, all of them revolving around the Sun. One group of rocky lumps never grew into planets and these are what we now term "asteroids."

ECLIPSE OF THE SUN

With all this movement going on, it is hardly surprising that sometimes one moon or planet will move in front of another. An eclipse of the Sun happens when the Moon comes between the Sun and the Earth. By chance, the Sun and the Moon appear to be exactly the same size in the sky — the Sun is much larger, of course, but the Moon looks the same size because it is much nearer. During an eclipse the Moon completely blocks out the Sun's light and its shadow falls on a small area of the Earth. When the whole of the Sun is hidden people see a total eclipse. This only lasts a few minutes. If the Moon covers only part of the Sun, however, this is called a partial eclipse.

While the Sun's bright disk is hidden, the thin gas of its outer atmosphere becomes visible as a shining halo.

This can only be seen during an eclipse because it is normally hidden by the Sun's brightness.

ECLIPSE OF THE MOON

An eclipse of the Moon happens when the Earth moves directly between the Sun and the Moon. The Moon travels through the Earth's shadow, sometimes turning a deep red color. A lunar eclipse may be total or partial, and a total eclipse can last for an hour or more.

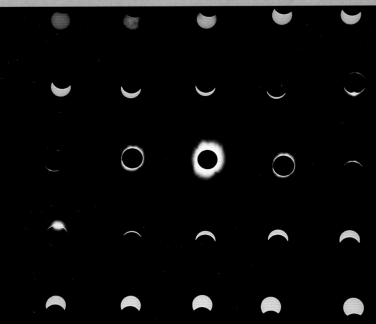

These pictures show an eclipse of the Sun as it happened. Starting at the top left corner, you can see the Moon covering more and more of the Sun. The middle picture shows a total eclipse when the Sun is completely hidden except for the glowing gas around it. A few minutes later the Sun begins to reappear from behind the Moon.

25

THE SUN

In the middle of the Solar System, holding it all together, is a star called the Sun. It is just an average star, like millions of others, not particularly big or bright. In fact it is a huge ball of hot, glowing gas and contains over 500 times as much material as the rest of the Solar System put together. To give an idea of its size, its diameter is about 109 times larger than that of the Earth.

The Sun is very hot — the temperature of the outer layer is about 10,800°F (6,000°C) — and sends out a constant flow of heat and light in every direction. This energy keeps all life on Earth alive — without it the Earth would be a cold, dark and lifeless ball of rock.

Where does all this energy come from? It is produced deep in the center of the Sun where the temperature is 27 million°F (15 million°C), much hotter than the Sun's surface. This is hot enough for atoms of hydrogen gas to combine to make another gas called helium. When this happens some of the Sun's material is turned into energy.

It is this energy that keeps the Sun shining. Every second, 4 million tons of the Sun's material is turned into energy. However, the Sun is so huge that it can go on shining just as it is now for about another 5 thousand million years before it runs out of fuel. It is already about 5 thousand million years old.

Astronomers term the yellow surface of the Sun the "photosphere." It is not as smooth as it may seem. Detailed photographs show that it has a mottled appearance called granulation. This is caused by columns of hot gas constantly rising to the surface. The gas then cools as it gives out heat and light and sinks back down again. So the surface is always moving, like a boiling liquid.

Above the surface, the gas thins out to become the Sun's atmosphere. There are two layers of atmosphere — the one nearer the Sun is called the chromosphere, and further out is the corona where the gas is much thinner. Some of it streams out away from the Sun and is called the solar wind. This travels right through the Solar System, beyond Pluto's orbit, becoming thinner as it spreads out.

SUNSPOTS, PROMINENCES AND FLARES

There are often disturbances on the surface of the Sun. Darker areas termed sunspots appear — they look dark because they are cooler than the rest of the surface, although they are still very hot. They usually appear in pairs or larger groups and can last for a few hours or for many months. Many are much larger than the Earth.

Prominences, such as the one shown on this page, can also sometimes be seen rising up above the Sun's surface into the corona. These are huge loops or tongues of cooler gas and look quite spectacular. Some hang above the surface, not seeming to move, for hours or even days. Others appear to surge upward very quickly, sometimes reaching heights of up to 600,000 miles (1 million km) above the Sun's surface.

There are also solar flares. Flares are extremely violent explosions above the Sun's surface, which throw out huge

Never look directly at the Sun, especially with binoculars or a telescope even with filters. It will make you go blind.

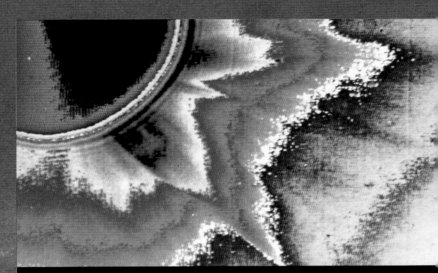

Colors have been added to this satellite picture of part of the Sun's corona — it would actually appear to be white. The circle at the upper left is the Sun itself.

amounts of energy. They may last only five or 10 minutes but give out the energy equivalent to about a million hydrogen bombs. Only a tiny fraction of this reaches the Earth but it is enough to cause interference with radio and television signals, as well as affecting electrical power supplies.

These sudden outbursts of extra energy make very little difference to the overall heat and light that the Sun steadily produces. While this continues, life on Earth will be able to flourish.

SUNSPOTS

Astronomers have records of sunspots going back to the year 1610. These show that the number of sunspots rises to a peak every 11 years. In between these peaks the number of sunspots drops to almost none. For some unexplained reason, there were no sunspot peaks between the years 1645 and 1715. Almost no sunspots were seen at all in this period. During those years, the weather was exceptionally cold, so cold that it was called the Little Ice Age. The River Thames in London regularly froze over, something it never does now. The ice was even thick enough to hold "Ice Fairs" on the river.

THE PLANETS

The four planets nearest to the Sun — Mercury, Venus, Earth, and Mars — are all hard, rocky balls. The next four — Jupiter, Saturn, Uranus, and Neptune — are quite different because they are made mainly of hydrogen in gas and liquid form, with only a small rocky core in the center. They do not have a solid surface that a spaceship could land on. They are termed the gas giants and are much bigger than the four rocky planets. They are much further apart and all have large families of moons circling around them. The most distant planet, Pluto, is the odd one out because it is very tiny and icy. In fact, it is not much like a planet at all because it is so small and because it has a moon almost as big as itself.

MERCURY

Mercury is the nearest planet to the Sun and is also the smallest, except for Pluto. Its diameter is only about half as big as that of the Earth. It can only be seen for a short

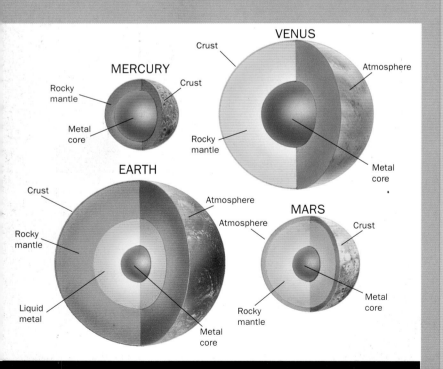

MERCURY
Rocky mantle
Crust
Metal core

VENUS
Crust
Atmosphere
Rocky mantle
Metal core

EARTH
Crust
Rocky mantle
Liquid metal
Atmosphere
Metal core

MARS
Atmosphere
Crust
Metal core
Rocky mantle

Earthquakes tell us that the Earth has a solid iron core, inside a molten iron layer. Next is a thick mantle of rock, with a thin rocky crust on the outside. The other rocky planets are probably similar.

DAYS AND YEARS

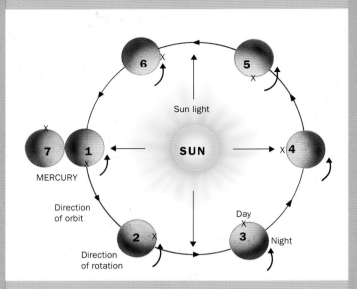

Sun light
SUN
6
5
7
1
MERCURY
X
4
Direction of orbit
2
3
Day
Night
Direction of rotation

A year on any planet is measured by the time it takes for the planet to circle around the Sun. On Earth, this is 365.25 days. So, the length of the year is different for each planet because they all take different times to circle around the Sun.

The length of the day is different for each planet as well. A day is the time between two sunrises or two sunsets, which is 24 hours on Earth. This is the same as the time it takes for the Earth to spin round once on its axis. On all the planets that spin round quickly, a day is the same as the time for one complete rotation. But this is not true for planets that spin round slowly, like Mercury and Venus. Their orbit round the Sun also affects the length of the day.

The diagram shows how Mercury spins round as it orbits the Sun. At each number the planet has completed one quarter of a spin. At 1, the time at the cross on the surface is sunrise. At 2, the time at the cross is early morning. At 3, after half a rotation, the time at the cross is still morning. At 4, the time is noon. At 5, after one complete rotation, the time is afternoon. At 6, it is late afternoon, and at 7 it is sunset. At this point Mercury has traveled right round the Sun, so a year has passed on Mercury. But from any point on the surface only half a day has passed. Mercury will spend another year going round the Sun again, before a complete day and night has finished.

time just before sunrise or after sunset because it is so close to the Sun. It is in the sky during the day when the sky is too light for Mercury to be seen clearly.

Mercury was named for the messenger of the gods because it moves so swiftly. It takes 88 Earth days to travel once round the Sun; this is its year. It takes nearly 59 days to spin once on its axis, but this is not the length of its day. In the time it takes to spin once it also travels two-thirds of its way round the Sun. This makes the time between two middays on Mercury 176 Earth days. So Mercury's day is twice as long as its year.

This long day means that the side of Mercury facing the Sun gets very hot. The temperature can reach 806°F (430°C), twice as hot as a hot oven. The side turned away from the Sun, where it is night, has time to cool down and get very cold indeed, –274°F (–170°C), which is much lower than the lowest temperatures on Earth. One reason for this is that Mercury has no atmosphere to hold the heat like a blanket.

Mercury is covered with craters of all sizes, made by rocks crashing onto the surface long ago. In fact, Mercury looks very like the Moon, but instead of the Moon's plains, it has huge cliffs. These seem to have been pushed up like wrinkles when the inside of Mercury cooled and shrank billions of years ago.

MARINER 10

Only one spacecraft, called Mariner 10, has been sent to visit Mercury. Mariner 10 flew past Mercury three times. Before its first visit in 1974, astronomers knew very little about the planet. Mariner 10 sent back close-up views of its cratered surface that could almost be mistaken for the Moon.

MERCURY	
Average distance from Sun	36 million miles (58 million km)
Time to orbit sun	88 days
Time to spin once	58.6 days
Average surface temperature	660 °F (350 °C) day –274 °F (–170 °C) night
No. of moons	0

Mercury's craters make it look like the Moon.

Craters are made by rocks speeding through space. When a rock crashes into the surface of a moon or planet it makes a circular dent and throws up a shower of shattered rock. This rock falls back, making a ring of mountains round the crater. Some of it slips down to fill the crater floor. If the rock is very large, the floor of the crater may "bounce back," throwing up a mountain in the middle of the crater. Even larger rocks produce craters with several rings of mountains.

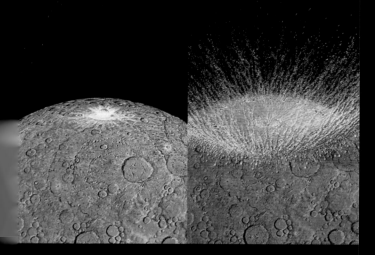

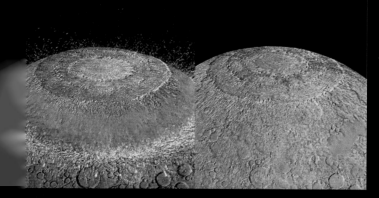

A rock from space crashing into a planet heats the planet's rocky surface so much that it melts, making a crater. Eventually, a mountain may form in the middle.

Venus is quite different from Mercury. It is easy to see in the sky because it is very bright — only the Sun and Moon are brighter than Venus. Perhaps its brilliance is the reason why it was named after the goddess of love. You can often see Venus as the "Evening Star," the first bright "star" to appear as the sky darkens after sunset. At other times Venus is the "Morning Star," shining brightly in the East just before sunrise. Of course, Venus is not really a star at all but a planet, just like the Earth.

Venus is often called the sister planet to the Earth. It is almost the same size as the Earth and the nearest planet to us. But thick clouds completely cover its surface, hiding a planet which is actually very different from the Earth. Venus spins very slowly and in the opposite direction to most of the other planets. It takes 243 Earth days to turn once and 225 Earth days to travel round the Sun. A day on Venus, from noon to noon, lasts approximately 117 Earth days.

The thick atmosphere makes Venus a very dangerous place to explore. This is because it mainly consists of a gas called carbon dioxide which we cannot breathe. It also traps the heat so that Venus is even hotter than Mercury. The atmosphere is so thick that it presses down 90 times harder than the air on Earth, and would immediately crush anyone who tried to land there. The thick clouds are also dangerous. They contain an acid called sulfuric acid which can burn your skin. Even the spacecraft specially built to land on Venus only survived for a short time.

Spacecraft pictures of Venus show a dry rocky surface. It seems to be mainly flat with some huge high plateaux and mountainous areas with large volcanoes. The largest

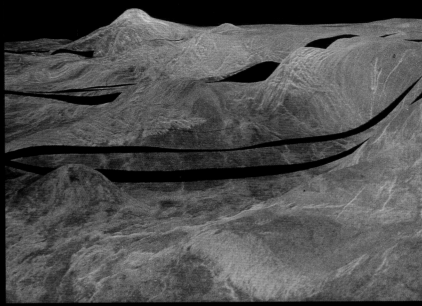

The Magellan spacecraft used radar to map the surface of Venus. A computer then made this picture of hills and a mountain. The black areas are where the spacecraft did not take any measurements.

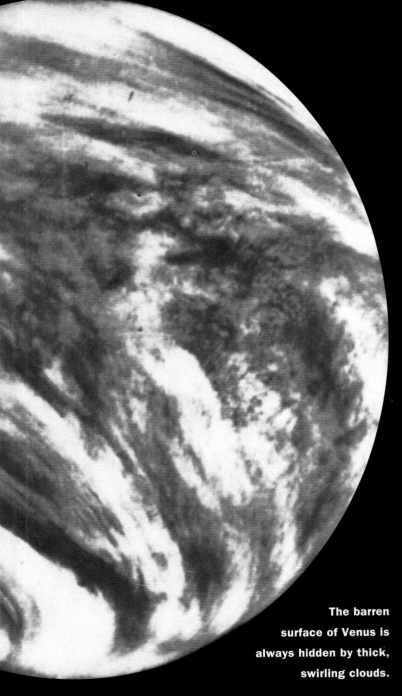

The barren surface of Venus is always hidden by thick, swirling clouds.

VENUS	
Average distance from Sun	67 million miles (108 million km)
Time to orbit Sun	225 days
Time to spin once	243 days
Average surface temperature	870 °F (465 °C)
No. of moons	0

than Mount Everest. Astronomers do not know if the volcanoes are still active or if they are extinct.

VISITING VENUS

Many spacecraft have been sent to explore Venus. The series of Russian Venera spacecraft that landed on the planet's surface in the 1970s only survived the heat and the crushing atmospheric pressure for a maximum of two hours. Fortunately, this was long enough for them to send back some close-up pictures of the surface.

The clouds have been explored by probes and balloons that took measurements as they floated down. The surface has also been mapped by spacecraft in orbit around Venus. These spacecraft have sent radio waves through the clouds to bounce back from the surface, showing the mountains, valleys, and craters below. In the 1990s the Magellan spacecraft has used radio waves to map the surface of Venus in great detail.

EARTH

Earth is a beautiful blue planet with white swirling clouds and is unique in many ways. It is the only planet in the Solar System where we know that there is life. It is also the only planet that has water on the surface — about two-thirds of the Earth is covered with oceans of water. In colder parts the water freezes into ice and there are droplets of water in the clouds.

The outer layers of the Earth that we live on seem to be solid and unmoving, but in fact the crust is made of separate pieces, termed plates, that move very gradually. In some places, the plates move apart and new rock pushes up from underneath to fill the gap. In other places, they push together and one plate slips down underneath another. Two plates pushing together are making mountain ranges like the Himalayas and the Alps. Other plates slide sideways against each other, causing earthquakes. Volcanoes erupt near the edges of the moving plates.

This means that the Earth's surface is slowly but constantly changing. For example, North America and Europe are moving apart by about four-fifths of an inch (20mm) every year. Earth is probably the only

EARTH	
distance from Sun	93 million miles (150 million km)
orbit Sun	365 1/4 days
spin once	24 hours
surface rature	59 °F (15 °C)
oons	1

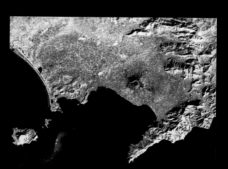

Above:
Looking at Earth from space, you can see white clouds, blue oceans, and land with trees, plants, and deserts. Left: This is a satellite view of the active volcano Vesuvius, in Italy.

rocky planet that has these moving plates.

The air on Earth is also different from the atmospheres of our nearest neighbours, Venus and Mars. Both of these planets are surrounded by gas which is mainly carbon dioxide, but the Earth's air has only tiny amounts of carbon dioxide. The Earth's atmosphere contains mainly nitrogen gas, and oxygen gas which we are able to breathe.

As the third planet, Earth is just the right distance from the Sun. It is not too hot like Mercury and Venus, or too cold like Mars. The temperature is just right to keep water flowing in rivers and seas. This is why there is so much life on Earth, but — as far as we know — nowhere else in the Solar System.

Below: From space you can see four giant volcanoes on the surface of Mars.

MARS

Average distance from Sun	142 million miles (228 million km)
Time to orbit Sun	687 days
Time to spin once	24 hours 37 minutes
Average surface temperature	−9 °F (−23 °C)
No. of moons	2

MARS

Mars looks red when you see it in the sky. It is often called the Red Planet and was named for the Roman god of war. Mars is much smaller than Earth or Venus — its diameter is only about half the Earth's. A day on Mars is almost the same time as on Earth, only 41 minutes longer, but the year on Mars, lasting 687 Earth days, is almost twice as long as ours.

For over 100 years people wondered if there was life on Mars. Through their telescopes, astronomers could see ice caps like the Arctic and Antarctic on Earth which got smaller during the Martian summer. They also saw its red appearance change and thought that this could be plants growing on the planet's surface.

CANALS ON MARS?

In 1877 an Italian astronomer called Giovanni Schiaparelli discovered what he thought were long straight lines on Mars. He called them channels, or "canali" in Italian. Some people thought that he had seen canals, and assumed that these had been built by intelligent Martians. The idea of Martian people was fascinating and also scary, but there was no need to worry. In the mid 1960s the first pictures sent back by the space probe Mariner 4 clearly proved that there were no canals or channels on Mars. The lines were not real at all, they had just been an optical illusion, probably caused by drifting Martian dust.

Spacecraft pictures have shown us that Mars has a dry rocky surface covered in rusty red dust. The dust blown up by the wind makes the sky look pink, not blue like the sky we see on Earth. There are craters and huge volcanoes, though these have probably been extinct for millions of years. The volcano called Olympus Mons is the largest in the Solar System.

Mars also has huge canyons. The largest canyon, Valles Marineris, stretches a quarter of the way round the planet. It is 3,100 miles (5,000 km) long — 10 times longer than the Grand Canyon.

A WET PAST?

Instead of "canals," spacecraft have found valleys on Mars that look like dried-up river beds. There is no water on Mars today because it is too cold. However, billions of years ago it may have been warm enough for rivers to flow, and for rain to fall on Mars.

Like Venus, the atmosphere contains mainly carbon dioxide gas, but it is much thinner than on Venus or even on Earth. There are a very few clouds in the sky and in the mornings there is mist in some of the valleys. However, the biggest clouds are made of dust. The winds whip the dust up from the surface, sometimes covering the whole of Mars. It is these dust clouds, not growing plants, that make Mars appear to change.

VIKING ON MARS

In 1976 two spacecraft, Viking 1 and 2, landed on Mars. Part of the spacecraft stayed in orbit around Mars, sending back detailed pictures of the whole surface. The landers sent pictures showing rocks lying on dusty soil, and sand dunes. Arms reached out from the landers to scoop up soil for testing in the spacecraft. The tests showed no sign of anything living on Mars.

A Viking spacecraft sitting on the rocky surface of Mars. The two spacecraft observed the weather, measuring the winds and temperatures. The dust and rocks on Mars are in fact a rusty red color.

THE GAS GIANTS

The next four planets beyond Mars are termed the "gas giants," and are made mainly of gas and liquid. There are two pairs of giant planets. The nearer two, Jupiter and Saturn, are much larger than the other two, Uranus and Neptune. This makes them different inside, though they all have deep cloudy atmospheres.

On Jupiter and Saturn the gases at the bottom of the atmospheres merge into a thick layer of liquid. Right at the center they have a layer of ice around a small rocky core. Uranus and Neptune also have rocky cores. But these are covered by a thick icy layer that stretches right up to the cloudy atmosphere.

Voyager 2 with pictures of the four planets that it visited. You can see Jupiter on the right, with Uranus and Neptune above Saturn on the left.

EXPLORING THE GAS GIANTS

In the 1980s Jupiter, Saturn, Uranus, and Neptune were all on one side of the Sun, roughly lined up, which only

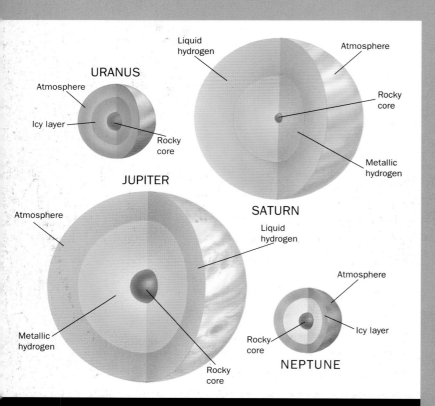

Deep inside Jupiter and Saturn it is believed that pressure is so great that the gas becomes like molten metal. Jupiter may have a rocky core about twice the size of the Earth.

happens once in about 175 years. This was a very good time to send a spacecraft to visit all four planets, one after another. So, in 1977 two Voyager spacecraft were launched from Earth toward the first gas giant, Jupiter.

They reached it nearly two years later in 1979, and went on to visit Saturn in 1980 and 1981. Voyager 1 then changed course to fly past Saturn's largest moon, Titan. After this, it started on an endless journey out of the Solar System toward the distant stars.

Voyager 2 continued its journey, reaching Uranus in 1986. Finally it flew past Neptune in 1989. The journey had taken 12 years altogether. During this time Voyager 2 had discovered new moons and rings around the planets and had sent astronomers huge amounts of new information about all the gas giants. Like Voyager 1, Voyager 2 is now on its way to the stars.

JUPITER

Jupiter is by far the biggest of all the planets. It is at least twice as massive as all the other planets put together. It is also very easy to see in the sky because it shines more brightly than any of the stars.

Jupiter is over five times as far from the Sun as the Earth and its year is almost 12 times as long as our year. Although it is so huge, Jupiter spins round in only 9 hours 50 minutes, so its day is less than half as long as ours. In

JUPITER

Average distance from Sun	483 million miles (778 million km)
Time to orbit Sun	11.9 years
Time to spin once	9 hours 50 minutes
Average surface temperature	–238 °F (–150 °C)
No. of moons	16

fact, it spins around so fast that it bulges out in the middle.

Like all the gas giants, the surface of Jupiter is not solid. We see the tops of its clouds which are spread out into dark and light bands by Jupiter's rapid spinning. The lighter bands of clouds are termed "zones." These are where warmer gases rise up above the other clouds. The darker cloud bands, termed "belts," are made of cooler gases that are sinking down. Close-up pictures from the Voyager spacecraft showed beautiful swirling patterns in the clouds. The tops of the clouds are very cold, about –238 °F (–150˚C), because Jupiter is such a long way from the Sun.

THE GREAT RED SPOT

In Jupiter's clouds there is a large red oval that was first seen over 300 years ago. It is called the Great Red Spot and seems to be a huge "storm," like a hurricane on Earth. It is a column of swirling cloud, more than twice as wide as the Earth. Nobody really knows why it is red. There are other, smaller, oval-shaped "storms" on Jupiter, both red and white, but none has lasted as long as the Great Red Spot.

SATURN

The second gas giant, Saturn, is nearly twice as far from the Sun as Jupiter. Saturn is a little smaller and spins round a little more slowly than Jupiter, making its day 10 hours 40 minutes long. This is still fast enough to produce a bulge in the middle — in fact, Saturn bulges more than any other planet.

Because it is so far from the Sun, Saturn's year is much longer than Jupiter's, nearly 30 Earth years long. Its distance from the Sun also makes Saturn a much colder planet. One difference between Saturn and all the other planets is that Saturn would float, like a cork, on water if you could find a sea large enough.

Saturn's clouds are stretched out into bands like those on Jupiter. Very strong winds blow along the bands, reaching speeds of over 1,100 miles (1,800km) an hour near Saturn's equator. The Voyager pictures also showed one storm like the Great Red Spot. This was named Anne's Spot, after the scientist, Anne Bunker, who discovered it.

A PLANET WITH HANDLES?

Although Saturn is bright enough to be seen in the sky quite easily, its spectacular rings can only be seen with a telescope. In 1610 Galileo looked at Saturn through his telescope and saw a bright spot on either side of the planet. He thought that Saturn had two companions. Other astronomers at that time drew pictures of Saturn looking as though it had handles, or even ears! Finally, in 1655, the astronomer Christiaan Huygens realized that what they had all seen was actually a ring around Saturn.

SATURN

Average distance from Sun	887 million miles (1,427 million km)
Time to orbit Sun	29.5 years
Time to spin once	10 hours 39 minutes
Average surface temperature	–290 °F (–180 °C)
No. of moons	19 +

These are both pictures of one of the smaller gas giant planets, Uranus. The one on the left is how an astronaut would see Uranus from a passing spacecraft — it would be completely covered with a plain blanket of blue-green clouds. The other picture has been colored using a computer to show up small differences in the cloud layer. These colors cannot be seen with the naked eye.

URANUS

Uranus is smaller than Jupiter and Saturn, but is still a giant compared to the Earth. Uranus is twice as far from the Sun as Saturn and, at this enormous distance, it takes 84 years to circle the Sun — since it was discovered in 1781 it has only completed two whole orbits around the Sun.

Like the other gas giants, Uranus spins very fast, taking only 17 hours 14 minutes. Uranus is very peculiar because it spins round as though it is lying on its side. It seems to be tipped up and "rolling" round the Sun. Its rings and moons are also tipped over in the same way.

This gives Uranus rather strange seasons. One pole faces the Sun and has constant sunlight for about 40 years. This end of the planet then goes into complete darkness for about another 40 years while the other pole of the planet faces the Sun.

The pictures of Uranus sent back by Voyager 2 in 1986 were not very exciting. They showed a smooth greeny-blue surface with no features or patterns, just a very few small white clouds. If there are any other cloud patterns, they must be hidden under a layer of haze that covers the whole planet.

DISCOVERING URANUS

Uranus is the first planet to be discovered since ancient times. It was discovered in 1781 by the astronomer, William Herschel. He was making a survey of stars in the sky when he noticed a greenish disk that was not a point of light like the stars. At first he thought he had found a comet, but later he realized that it was not moving like a comet, so it must be a new planet. Although Herschel wanted to name it for King George of England, it was finally named Uranus for the ancient Greek god.

URANUS	
Average distance from Sun	1,783 million miles (2,870 million km)
Time to orbit Sun	84 years
Time to spin once	17 hours 14 minutes
Average surface temperature	−346 °F (−210 °C)
No. of moons	15

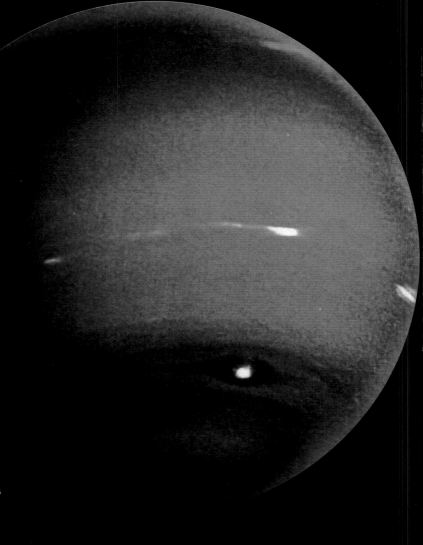

NEPTUNE

Neptune is a similar planet to Uranus, though it is not tipped over on its side and is a little smaller than Uranus. A day on Neptune lasts 16 hours 3 minutes, still less than a day on Earth. Neptune is about 2.8 billion miles (4.5 billion km) from the Sun, so it takes about 165 years to circle round it once.

When Voyager 2 reached Neptune in 1989 it found a very blue planet with streaks of white clouds. Like Jupiter, Neptune has a spot, although Neptune's is darker. There is also a smaller dark spot that turns around in the opposite direction to the larger one.

Both of the spots are swept along by winds blowing as fast as 1,300 miles (2,100 km) an hour — the fastest winds in the Solar System. The Voyager scientists named one white cloud on Neptune the Scooter, because it seems to scoot round the planet overtaking the dark spots.

DISCOVERING NEPTUNE

Astronomers noticed that the newly discovered planet

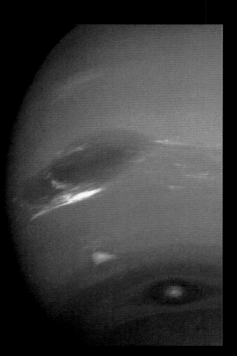

Here you can see the Great Dark Spot. This is a huge, oval-shaped storm that swirls around in Neptune's bright blue cloud layer. Smaller white and wispy clouds float above the blue clouds and the Great Dark Spot. Near the bottom of the picture you can also see the Scooter. This is a larger white cloud that always seems to be racing around the planet.

Uranus did not move as they expected. They thought that it was being pulled out of its orbit by something further from the Sun, possibly by another, as yet unknown, planet. In the early 1800s, two young astronomers, John Couch Adams in England and Urbain Leverrier in France, separately worked out where this new planet should be. Neptune was actually found by Johann Galle of Berlin, Germany, in 1846, almost exactly where both calculations said it should be.

NEPTUNE	
Average distance from Sun	2,794 million miles (4,497 million km)
Time to orbit Sun	164.8 years
Time to spin once	16 hours 3 minutes
Average surface temperature	–364 °F (–220 °C)
No. of moons	8

PLUTO

Average distance from Sun	3,666 million miles (5,913 million km)
Time to orbit Sun	248 years
Time to spin once	6 days 9 hours
Average surface temperature	−382 °F (−230 °C)
No. of moons	1

PLUTO

Pluto, the furthest planet from the Sun, is an oddity. It is the smallest of all the planets, smaller than our Moon and less than half as big as the largest moons in the Solar System. Pluto's orbit is not very like those of the other planets either, as it is tilted and more elongated. This sometimes brings Pluto closer to the Sun than Neptune. In fact, between 1977 and 1999, Neptune is the most distant planet. Although their orbits cross, there is little danger of the two planets colliding.

We do not know very much about Pluto because it is very small and very far away — so far that it takes 248 years to travel round the Sun. Its day is almost 6.5 times as long as ours. Pluto is the only planet that has never been visited by a space probe from Earth. It probably has a rocky center covered by a thick layer of ice. It seems to have a very thin atmosphere but only when its orbit brings it closer to the Sun.

DISCOVERING PLUTO

After Neptune was discovered, astronomers thought that Uranus still seemed to be pulled off course, so maybe there was another unknown planet beyond Neptune. Percival Lowell was one astronomer who searched for this new planet, but did not find anything. However, 14 years after Lowell died, Pluto was finally found by an astronomer working at Lowell's observatory in America. In 1930, Clyde Tombaugh was comparing two photographs of the sky when he noticed that one of the stars had moved slightly. This was not a star at all — it was Pluto.

PLANET X

Pluto is much too small to have pulled Uranus off course, so astronomers are looking for yet another planet even further away than Pluto. They call it Planet X. It would not be easy to find, because at this distance from the Sun there is very little sunlight for the planet to reflect and so it would be very hard to see. Scientists are now tracking the four spacecraft that are heading away from the Solar System but have not yet found anything. If one of them passes a large planet, it would be pulled off course.

This painting gives us an idea of what Pluto and its moon, Charon, probably look like. Charon is not much smaller than Pluto and they circle around each other. For this reason, Pluto and Charon are sometimes called a "double planet." Because they are right at the edge of the Solar System, they receive very little light or heat from the Sun. This means that they are very cold indeed.

PLANETS WITH MOONS

Only Mercury and Venus have no moons at all. Earth and Pluto each have one moon; Mars has two small moons; and the gas giants have large families of moons, like miniature solar systems — of these, Saturn has the most with about 19 moons. There is a list of all these moons at the back of this book.

Apollo astronaut John Young standing near his Lunar Module on the dry and dusty surface of the Moon. Astronauts need spacesuits to supply them with air to breathe. This is because, unlike the Earth, the Moon has no atmosphere of its own.

THE MOON

The Earth's Moon is the fifth largest moon in the Solar System. Its diameter is about a quarter of the Earth's. It is a dry and dusty place, covered with craters of many different sizes. There are also large, dark plains that astronomers in the past thought were seas. Although we now know that there is no water at all on the Moon, these plains are still called "seas." They look dark because they were covered with lava from volcanoes that erupted billions of years ago.

There is no atmosphere on the Moon so there is no wind or rain to weather the surface. The rocks and dust on the Moon will therefore remain exactly the same for millions of years, except where they are disturbed by astronauts from Earth.

The Moon circles round the Earth in about 27 days. It also spins round in exactly the same time, so the same side of the Moon always faces the Earth. No-one on Earth had ever seen the other side of the Moon until 1959 when a Russian spacecraft, Luna 3, flew behind the Moon. Its pictures showed many craters just like the ones on the side we can see, but there are no large "seas." Since then the Moon has been explored by many space probes and the whole surface has been mapped using pictures taken by orbiting spacecraft.

In 1969 the first Apollo astronauts landed on the Moon. Altogether there were six Apollo Moon landings, each in a different area. They brought samples of Moon rock back to Earth for scientists to study, and left experiments on the Moon. The Moon is still the only place in the Solar System that has been visited by people from Earth.

PHASES OF THE MOON

The Moon looks as though it changes shape in the sky. It seems to grow from a thin crescent to a full disk, then shrink again to a crescent. This is because the Moon shines by reflecting sunlight. The Moon itself does not change, but we can only see the part of the Moon that is lit by the Sun, so as it moves round the Earth we see different amounts of the sunlit side. When the sunlit side faces the Earth, there is a full Moon. When the sunlit side is facing almost completely away from the Earth, we only see a thin crescent. These changes are termed the phases of the Moon.

MOONS OF MARS

Mars has two very tiny moons — Phobos and Deimos — their names mean "fear" and "panic" in Greek! They are roughly oval-shaped and covered with craters. The largest is only 17 miles (28km) long. They may have been asteroids that were captured by the pull of Mars' gravity and then became its moons.

JUPITER'S MOONS

Jupiter has 16 moons. There are four large ones, Io, Europa, Ganymede, and Callisto. These are also called the Galilean moons, for Galileo, the 17th century scientist. They were one of the first discoveries that Galileo made when he started looking at the sky through a telescope in 1610. Ganymede is the largest moon in the Solar System.

Io is a very strange moon. It looks like a pizza, with blotchy red, orange and yellow areas, and is dotted with volcanoes that are constantly erupting. Some of these throw plumes of material hundreds of miles high above the surface. The rest of Jupiter's moons are all small and icy.

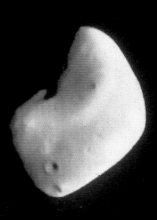

Compared to most of the other moons, the two moons of Mars seem tiny. They are called Phobos and Deimos. They are not round, like the Earth's Moon, but are shaped like potatoes! Phobos is much closer to Mars than Deimos and races around the planet in about 7.5 hours.

SATURN'S MOONS

Saturn has about 19 moons, more than any other planet. Many of them are small and icy, but the largest, Titan, is the second largest in the Solar System. Titan has a very thick atmosphere, thicker than that on Earth, and has clouds that completely hide its surface. Two of Saturn's small moons named Janus and Epimetheus seem to have been made from a larger moon that split in half.

URANUS' MOONS

Uranus has about 15 moons. Of this total, 10 were discovered by the spacecraft Voyager 2 in 1986. These new, recently discovered moons are all very small and very dark. They reflect very little of the weak sunlight that reaches them. The two largest moons, on the other hand, were discovered by William Herschel just a few years after he had discovered the planet itself.

Miranda, the smallest of the five large moons, looks very strange. It has areas with craters, and huge cliffs and grooves all mixed together. Scientists think it may have been hit by a large rock that split it apart. The separate chunks later joined up again haphazardly.

Right: These pictures of Saturn and six of its moons were all taken separately by the Voyager spacecraft, as it sped past each in turn.

The main picture shows four of the largest moons of Uranus: Ariel (left of Uranus), Miranda (right of Uranus), Oberon above, and Titania far right.

Jupiter with its four largest moons: Io,
Europa, Ganymede, and Callisto.

NEPTUNE'S MOONS

Voyager 2 also discovered six new moons around Neptune in 1989, making about eight in all. There is only one large moon, called Triton, and it is the coldest place in the Solar System. It travels around Neptune in the opposite direction to all the other moons. It has a very thin atmosphere, and what seem to be active volcanoes. They throw up dusty material that is blown sideways by the wind, looking like dark streaks on the surface.

CHARON

Even tiny Pluto has a moon, called Charon. It was only discovered in 1978 and was not officially named until 1985. Charon is about half as big as Pluto and travels around Pluto in about 6.5 days. Pluto spins round in exactly the same time. This means that Charon would always appear in the same position in Pluto's sky. From the other side of Pluto, Charon would never be seen at all.

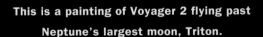

This is a painting of Voyager 2 flying past Neptune's largest moon, Triton.

45

The Galileo spacecraft is due to arrive at Jupiter in 1995. It will drop a probe into the planet's atmosphere and spend nearly two years studying Jupiter. The picture shows what it may look like.

PLANETS WITH RINGS

Astronomers have known that Saturn was surrounded by brilliant rings ever since 1655. Much more recently, however, since 1977, smaller rings have also been found around all the other gas giants. None of the small rocky planets, like the Earth or Mars, have rings.

The rings around gas giants are not solid, but are made of millions of separate pieces of ice and rock, all circling round the planet. The size of the pieces varies enormously. Some of them can be as small as tiny dust particles, while others are large boulders, some larger than a house.

Uranus has 11 narrow rings made of a very dark material, almost as black as coal. These were first discovered in 1977. Astronomers were watching as Uranus moved in front of a bright star. They were surprised to see the star "blink" on and off several times before it disappeared behind the planet. Each ring had briefly blocked out the light from the star.

Voyager 2 discovered rings around Neptune in 1989, although they are much fainter than those found around Uranus. There are four rings made of fine dark dust. Surprisingly, one of Neptune's rings is uneven, with thicker clumps of dust in three places. Voyager also discovered Jupiter's very faint ring.

SATURN'S RINGS

Saturn is surrounded by a magnificent set of bright shining rings. They stretch out around its equator,

The colors added to this picture of Saturn's rings show up the differences in their icy chunks.

reaching further from the planet than the width of the planet itself. They are about 43,500 miles (70,000km) wide but extremely thin — less than half a mile. The pieces of ice and icy rock in the rings reflect the sunlight, making them shine brilliantly.

From Earth astronomers can see three rings, which they call A, B and C. There seems to be a gap between A and B. This was first seen in 1675 by Cassini and is called the Cassini Division for him. When the Voyager spacecraft visited Saturn, they discovered that the rings were much more complicated than expected. They also discovered four more rings, and found that the main rings contained thousands of tiny ringlets. There were even some ringlets within the Cassini Division.

ASTEROIDS

As well as the nine main planets, the Solar System also has a collection of minor planets. They circle the Sun mainly in an area between the orbits of Mars and Jupiter, called the asteroid belt. The largest, Ceres, is about 620 miles (1,000km) across. However, most are much smaller than this. Ceres was the first asteroid to be discovered, by Giuseppe Piazza in 1801. Like Uranus, Ceres was mistaken for a comet at first.

Nobody knows how many asteroids there are because most are much too small to be seen from the Earth. There may be as many as half a million that measure half a mile or more across, and many more smaller ones. Although

In 1993 the Galileo spacecraft sent back this close-up picture of the asteroid called Ida. It is only about 50km (31 miles) long and is covered in very old craters.

there are so many, they are well spread out in space, with millions of miles between them.

Asteroids are just chunks of rock, but they are not all made from the same type of rock. Most are made of very dark rock and are termed carbonaceous. Others, termed stony asteroids, are greyish in color, while a third type are mainly made of metal.

Halley's comet when it returned to the Sun in 1986. The colors show the different temperatures in the tail.

COMETS

Another collection of small objects in the Solar System are comets. They are too small and dim to be seen with a telescope, except when near the Sun. Then they develop shining tails that are sometimes bright enough to be seen without a telescope. They come from the edges of the Solar System, and swing close to the Sun before disappearing again. Astronomers think comets may come from a huge cloud of comets called the Oort Cloud around the edge of the Solar System.

Comets are made of a mixture of dust and ice, rather like dirty snowballs. As they come near the Sun, some ice melts, making a huge glowing cloud of gas and dust around the comet. This cloud is termed the head or coma, and the solid part in the middle is the nucleus.

The solar wind from the Sun blows the gas and dust out into a magnificent tail. This always points away from the Sun, so when the comet is moving away from the Sun it goes tail first. There are often two tails, one of dust and one of gas. The dust tail is curved and appears yellow because the dust reflects the sunlight. The gas tail is straighter and shines because the gas is glowing. Although a comet's nucleus is usually under 6 miles (10km) long, the head can be about 600,000 miles (one million km) across. Comet tails may be hundreds of millions of miles long.

COMETS AND SHOOTING STARS

Comets leave a trail of dust behind them. During the year the Earth regularly passes through these dust trails. At these times showers of meteors are seen. Meteors are just dust grains burning up when they hit the top of our atmosphere. The dust becomes very hot as it rubs against the atmosphere, so hot that it burns away. The air around these particles also becomes hot enough to glow, and we see this as a streak of light in the sky that disappears almost immediately. This streak of light is called a meteor, or more often a shooting star.

Shooting stars can happen at any time, whenever a

Most of the time a comet is just a chunk of dust and ice (as shown on the left). However, when it comes near the Sun, the ice starts to melt, making a cloud of gas (as shown in the middle). This gas is blown out into a tail (as shown on the right).

HALLEY'S COMET AND GIOTTO

The most famous comet of all is Halley's Comet, whose orbit round the Sun brings it back about every 76 years. The last time it returned was in 1986 and the next will be in 2061. It was named for Edmond Halley, who realized that three comets seen in 1531, 1607 and 1682 could be different visits from the same comet. He predicted when it would next return and it arrived on time, though he did not live long enough to see it.

When Halley's Comet returned in 1986 it was met by five spacecraft. One of them, Giotto, from Europe, flew through the comet's head, only 370 miles (600 km) from the nucleus. Its pictures gave astronomers their first view of a comet's nucleus. It was shaped like a potato, about 10 miles (16 km) long, and was very dark with bright areas where plumes of dust were escaping. Each time it passes the Sun, Halley's Comet loses about 250 million tons of material, but it is big enough to last for thousands of years yet.

The Meteor Crater in Arizona was made when a huge rock from space crashed into the Earth, probably about 50,000 years ago. It looks very much like the craters we can see on the Moon.

the fine dust is too small to burn. It is just scooped up by the Earth and gently sinks down to the ground. It is estimated that the Earth may scoop up about 100 tons of space dust every day.

METEORITES

Meteorites are large chunks of rock that do not burn up completely when they hit the Earth's atmosphere. They become very hot and glow as a bright fireball, but they are not destroyed and fall down to hit the ground.

Luckily no-one has been killed by a falling meteorite. The largest one found on Earth is in Namibia, Africa. It is still in the ground where it originally fell and probably weighs about 55 tons.

Meteorites seem to be made of the same materials

as the asteroids. Scientists think that they may be the pieces which are broken off when asteroids bump into each other. The pieces shoot out in all directions, some on a collision course with the Earth.

CRATERS AND EXPLOSIONS

Very large meteorites hit the ground hard enough to make craters like the ones on the Moon. The most famous meteorite crater on Earth is in Arizona. It measures about half a mile (1 km) across and is thought to be about 50,000 years old. The meteorite that made it must have weighed about 10,000 tons. It was destroyed when it hit the ground, leaving only scattered fragments. In this century there have been two large meteorite falls, both in wilderness areas in Siberia.

There was a deafening explosion and a fireball as bright as the Sun. There was no crater because the meteorite (which may have been a small comet) exploded up in the atmosphere, but the forest was flattened for about 18 miles (30km) around. In 1947 another fireball was seen near Vladivostock. This time there were over a hundred craters and tons of meteorite pieces were found.

EETA790C

This meteorite is a rock from space which fell to Earth. It was found in Antarctica.

3

INSIDE OUR GALAXY

You only have to look up at the sky at night to see that the Earth is surrounded by stars. If you are in a very dark place, you should be able to see over 2,000 stars without using a telescope or binoculars. All these stars, including the Sun, are part of a huge family of stars, called the Galaxy. There are more than one hundred billion stars in the Galaxy as well as clouds of gas and dust. From Earth we can see part of our Galaxy in the night sky. It is the faint band of light across the sky that we call the Milky Way. You can only see it on a really clear moonless night, and you need to get well away from the dazzling glow of street or house lights.

All these stars and the dark patches of dust are part of our Galaxy.

ALL KINDS OF STARS

There are many different kinds of stars in our Galaxy such as binary stars, variable stars, white dwarfs, and giant stars. All stars are huge balls of hot glowing gases. They shine because they make energy right at their cores, just like the Sun. They send out light in all directions and it is this starlight that we see when we look at the sky.

If you take a quick look at the night sky the stars look like points of light. However, you can see that some are brighter than others. You can also see that some stars are different colors.

You can see the different colors of the stars, some yellow, some red, in this small galaxy called Leo 1 near to our own.

BRIGHT STARS

There are two reasons why a star may look very bright. It may be very large and giving out a lot of light. On the other hand a smaller star, giving out less light, will also look bright if it is close to the Earth. The Sun is just an average star, not particularly bright, but it is overwhelmingly the brightest star in the Earth's sky because it is so much nearer to us than all the others.

The brightest star in the night sky is called Sirius, or the Dog Star. It actually gives out 26 times more light than the Sun. This is partly because it is a bigger, more powerful star, and partly because it is also one of the closest stars to us. However, it is so much further away than the Sun that, like all the other stars, it just looks like a twinkling point of light.

Another bright star called Rigel, in the constellation of Orion, actually gives out even more light than Sirius, over 2,000 times more light, but it does not look as bright as Sirius in the sky because it is 100 times further away.

BLUE, YELLOW, RED STARS

Stars have different colors and this difference is more noticeable if you look at them through binoculars. Stars are different colors because they have different temperatures. The Sun's surface temperature is about 11,000°F (6,000 °C), and it shines with a yellow light. Cooler stars with temperatures as low as 4,500 °F (2,500 °C) are a duller red. Hotter stars that glow white have surface temperatures around 18,000°F (10,000 °C). Even hotter are the very bright stars that look almost blue. These have a surface temperature of 45,000°F (25,000 °C) and over.

HOW BIG ARE THE STARS?

Stars in the sky do not always look very different in size, but in fact they come in a huge range of sizes from dwarfs to giants. The Sun is a fairly average-sized star, with a diameter of about 870,000 miles (1.4 million km), over 100 times larger than the Earth. At the end of its life it will become a white dwarf star, only about the size of the Earth. This happens to all ordinary stars like our Sun.

White dwarfs are so small that they can only be seen with powerful telescopes and then only if they are fairly close to the Sun. There are other even smaller stars, termed neutron stars, that can be as small as 6 miles (10 km) across — we will find out about them later in this chapter.

At the other end of the range are the giant stars, which have diameters up to 100 times larger than the Sun's diameter. Supergiant stars are even bigger, about 500 times larger than the Sun. These enormous stars give out thousands of times more light than the Sun and can be seen shining brightly in the sky.

Although they are easier to see, giant stars are not very common. The most common stars are ones about the size of the Sun.

Sirius is the brightest star in the sky. It is hotter than the Sun and shines a bright bluish white compared with the yellow of the Sun. Sirius has a companion star, a tiny white dwarf star, much too small to be seen without a telescope. The two stars take 50 years to circle around each other.

The spin of the Earth makes the stars look like streaks, and brings the Sun into the sky at dawn.

CHANGING STARS

The Sun shines very steadily, giving out the same amount of light and heat year after year. Stars that do not shine steadily like the Sun are called "variable" stars. Some vary with a regular pattern, getting brighter and then dimmer every few hours, days or weeks. Sometimes this is because a star actually swells up and then shrinks again — it looks brighter when it is bigger and dimmer when it is smaller.

Stars termed novae (which means "new") suddenly flare up extremely brightly then fade back again to normal. This is caused by a huge explosion on the surface of the star. Sometimes a whole star explodes. This is termed a supernova, and may happen when a huge giant star ends its life.

We are fortunate that the Sun is not a variable star. If it were, life on Earth could not survive because the temperature would be always changing from freezing cold to baking hot. The Sun has been shining now for about five billion years, providing just the right conditions for life to develop and flourish. It is still only in the middle of its life, and should not change much for the next four or five billion years.

GROUPS OF STARS

Only about half the stars we can see in the sky are single stars like the Sun. Most stars are in groups of two or more stars. In these groups the stars are close enough for their gravity to hold them together, so they circle around each other in space. Pairs of stars are termed double or binary stars. Some stars that seem to be variable are really two stars circling around each other. When one star passes in front of the other, the brightness of the double star changes.

MOVING STARS

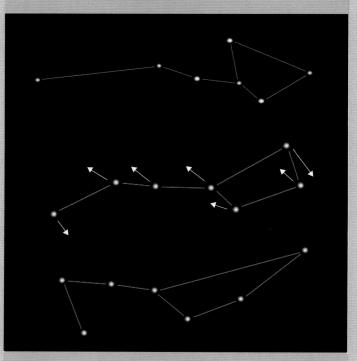

The patterns made by the stars in the sky, termed the constellations, never seem to change. However, minor changes do take place. The stars are actually moving fast through space, but this is very difficult to see because they are so far away. It will take many tens of thousands of years for the patterns of the constellations as we see them now to change noticeably.

For example, the constellation called the Plough (part of the Great Bear) is changing because two of the seven main stars are moving in the opposite direction to the others. If you look at the middle diagram the arrows show you which way the stars are moving. The top diagram shows you how the Great Bear would have looked 100,000 years ago, the middle diagram shows you how it looks today, and the bottom diagram shows how it will look in 100,000 years time.

This yellow star and its white dwarf companion are circling around each other, making a binary star.

A STAR IS BORN

Stars are born in the middle of huge clouds of gas and dust in space. These clouds are termed nebulae. A star starts to form when dust and gas begin to clump together in the nebulae. Gravity pulls the gas and dust closer together until eventually it collapses into a spinning ball of gas. In the middle of this, the material is pulled so tightly together that it starts to heat up. It grows hotter and hotter until eventually it starts to glow. This is not a real star yet; it is termed a protostar.

These protostars shine but they are hidden inside the cloud of dust and gas where they formed. They go on gradually shrinking and getting hotter. After millions of years, the core is hot enough for the atoms of hydrogen gas to combine to make helium gas. Now they are proper stars, making energy and giving out the starlight that we can see.

THE ADULT STAR

Once it has started producing energy, a star will not change much for millions or thousands of millions of years. It will just shine steadily so long as there is a

Above: A globular cluster contains hundreds and thousands of old stars.

Above: The Jewel Box is a good name for this open
cluster of bright, young stars which were probably
born in the same nebula.

supply of hydrogen gas at the core to produce energy.
Eventually this gas is used up.

The time this takes depends on the size of the star.
Smaller stars live longer than larger ones, because the
larger stars make much more energy and use up their
hydrogen much more quickly. Even though they have
more fuel to start with, they run out more quickly. Very
large stars may only shine steadily for millions of years.
Smaller stars start with less hydrogen gas but use it up
much more slowly, so they can go on shining for billions of
years. The Sun's lifetime will be about 10 billion years
altogether, and smaller stars will live even longer.

Left: New stars are being born within this
beautiful glowing cloud of gas and dust called
the Rosette Nebula.

DEATH OF A STAR

When a star has used up the hydrogen gas in its core and cannot make any more energy it starts to die. What happens next depends on how big the star is.

Let us look first at an average star about the size of the Sun. When this star stops making energy, its core starts to shrink. At the same time, the outer part of the star swells up, becomes cooler and changes from yellow to red. It becomes a red giant star. (The Sun may swell up to a hundred times its present size, and swallow up the nearest planets, which are Mercury and Venus. Its outside edge may even reach the Earth, but this will not happen for billions of years.)

This red giant star may pulse in and out, and this will make it a variable star for a while. Then some of the outside layer of gas will drift off into space. This makes a glowing shell of gas around the star termed a planetary nebula. Soon this gas will merge into the rest of the gas and dust between the stars.

All that is left of the original star is the hot core that has shrunk down until it is about the size of the Earth. It is very hot and shines as a tiny white star termed a white dwarf. It no longer makes any energy, so very gradually it cools and fades, changing from white to yellow to red until it stops shining altogether.

DEATH OF A MASSIVE STAR

A huge star, containing at least eight times more material than the Sun, will end its life with a gigantic explosion. It has had a short life of only a few million years, shining brightly as a blue giant star, but when its hydrogen fuel is used up it swells up into a red giant star, just like the smaller stars.

The core of the star shrinks and becomes hotter. In a giant star the core gets hot enough for the atoms of gas to combine to make other new materials including carbon, oxygen, and iron. While this is happening the star is making energy and is still shining. It stops making energy when the central core contains mainly iron. The core collapses very suddenly, in less than a

The Helix Nebula is a planetary nebula, a shell of glowing gas around a dying star.

The Vela supernova is the remains of an exploding supergiant star.

Left: You can see the dying star in the middle of this planetary nebula called the Dumbbell Nebula. The glowing gas cloud was originally part of this star. The cloud is beginning to fade and will eventually become invisible like most of the gas and dust between the stars.

second, and starts a violent explosion. The whole star, except the collapsed core, is thrown outward and destroyed.

This explosion is termed a supernova. For a short time the star may shine brighter than a billion suns — it can even outshine the galaxy in which it lives. The material thrown out by the explosion makes a shell of gas, which expands outward, bumping into the gas and dust in space. Astronomers can see these huge glowing clouds of gas, which they term supernova remnants. One famous supernova remnant is called the Crab Nebula because of its strange shape. The explosion that threw out this glowing cloud was seen nearly a thousand years ago in 1054. It was seen by Chinese astronomers and was so bright that it could be seen in the daylight sky for three weeks.

Eventually, the supernova remnant will merge into the surrounding gas and dust. The new materials made in the star and in the explosion may become part of a cloud where new stars are born, so the material of old stars is recycled to make new young stars. The Solar System must be made of these recycled materials because the planets contain material that could only have been made inside giant stars or in supernova explosions. You could say that the Earth is made of stardust!

NEUTRON STARS AND PULSARS

What happens to the core of a supernova during its catastrophic explosion? Surprisingly, it survives and collapses down to a very tiny star, even smaller than a white dwarf, measuring about 6 miles (10 km) across. It is termed a neutron star because it is made almost entirely of atomic particles called neutrons. It is packed so tightly together that a teaspoonful would weigh a 100 million tons. Astronomers cannot see the actual neutron stars because they are so tiny, but radio telescopes can detect radio pulses from spinning neutron stars. They term these pulsars.

The first pulsar was discovered by Jocelyn Bell in Cambridge, England, in 1967. She was using a radio telescope and noticed a series of regular blips coming from one part of the sky. At first astronomers wondered if an alien was sending us a message from outer space, but then other pulsars were found. The pulses of radio waves seemed to be coming from something that was spinning very fast and was so tiny it could only be a neutron star.

The neutron star gives out two narrow beams of radio waves, or sometimes light or x-rays. As the star spins around, the beams swing across the sky rather like a lighthouse beam. If the beam happens to point in our direction we observe a flash each time it swings around, so the telescope picks up a series of regular flashes. There are pulsars in the middle of several supernova remnants. The pulsar in the middle of the Crab Nebula gives out flashes of light and x-rays as well as radio waves.

Cygnus X-1 is the name given to a mysterious object that could be a black hole. Astronomers cannot actually see Cygnus X-1. It was discovered by an x-ray satellite telescope because it gives out very strong x-rays. They know that Cygnus X-1 is close to a giant star, and that it is very small but it contains at least ten times as much material as the Sun. Therefore it is very likely that the x-rays come from gas that is rapidly spiraling around a black hole just before being swallowed up. Astronomers also think that there may be much bigger black holes at the center of many galaxies, possibly even our own Galaxy. They term them super-massive black holes. These may even swallow whole stars that get too close. They would be ripped apart before they fell into the black hole.

BLACK HOLES

Neutron stars contain about two to three times as much material as the Sun, all in a ball about 6 miles (10 km) across. If the core left after a supernova explosion contains more than three times as much material as the Sun, it cannot become a neutron star. The core goes on collapsing. Its material is condensed into a smaller and smaller space and, as this happens, its own gravity becomes so strong that nothing can escape from it, not even light. It becomes a black hole in space. Nothing that falls into a black hole can ever escape. Since light cannot leave a black hole, we cannot even see it, neither can we know what is inside one nor what happens to something that falls into a black hole.

If we cannot see a black hole, how do we know that there are such things? Astronomers cannot be certain, but they are fairly sure that they do exist. Although they cannot see a black hole directly, they can see the effect one has on nearby objects. If one of a pair of stars happens to be a black hole, its strong pull of gravity may pull gas away from the other star. The gas circles round the hole, getting faster and hotter as it spirals and eventually becomes so hot that it gives out x-rays just before finally disappearing altogether.

Astronomers think they have found places in space where this is happening. They have discovered x-rays coming from a point, called Cygnus X-1, close to a large blue star, but they cannot see what is actually producing the x-rays. They know it is very small but that it contains at least ten times as much material as the Sun. The invisible "star" could be a black hole.

NEBULAE

As we have seen earlier, clouds of dust and gas are very important in the lives of stars. They begin their lives in these nebulae and at the end of their lives they leave behind new nebulae.

There are three main reasons why astronomers can see nebulae. Some are glowing clouds, others reflect starlight, while a third kind appear dark by blocking out starlight from stars behind them. When we see glowing nebulae it is often because light from bright young stars in or near the clouds is making the gas glow. These kind of nebulae usually look red or pink in photographs because the clouds are made mainly of hydrogen gas which glows red. An example of this is the Orion Nebula.

DUSTY CLOUDS

Often there are dark patches in the glowing cloud. This is where dust in the cloud is blocking out the light from the glowing clouds and stars behind it.

Large dark clouds are termed dark nebulae and can only be seen because they show up as a dark shape silhouetted against a glowing cloud or a starry background. Other dusty clouds can be seen as reflection nebulae. In these, the starlight from bright stars is reflected or scattered by the dust in the cloud. We see the scattered light as a blue glow around the star. It looks blue because the dust scatters blue light more than the other colors in starlight. Glowing, reflection and dark nebulae can be different parts of the same cloud.

The Orion Nebula is a huge cloud of glowing gas where new stars are being born. It is these bright young stars that make the gas glow.

You can see why this dark nebula is called the Horsehead Nebula. The dark shape of a horse's head shows up against the glowing nebula behind it. Both the dark and bright clouds are part of a huge cloud, much of which is invisible. This cloud also includes the bright Orion Nebula.

OUR GALAXY

All the stars you can see in the sky without a telescope are in our own Galaxy termed the Milky Way. There are over a hundred billion stars of all different kinds in our Galaxy. The Galaxy is termed a spiral galaxy because it has arms that curl round in a spiral shape coming out from a central bulge.

There are four main arms spiraling out from the middle of our Galaxy. They contain stars of all different types and different ages. Many of these are young and bright. There is also a large quantity of gas and dust among the stars in the spiral arms, which, as we have seen, is the material from which new stars are made.

The stars in the central bulge are all older. There is almost no gas and dust from which to make new stars. Stars in the central bulge are also much closer together than they are in the arms.

Astronomers think that the whole Galaxy began as a huge ball of gas. Because it was spinning around and around, the ball of gas gradually flattened out into a disk shape. The stars that had already formed stayed where they were, making a halo of older stars and globular clusters around the Galaxy. The gas flattened into the spiral arms where stars are still being born today.

The blue glow around the brilliant young stars of the Pleiades is dust reflecting the starlight. This is a reflection nebula.

CIRCLING AROUND OUR GALAXY

All the stars in the spiral arms are orbiting around the middle of the Galaxy. The Sun will take about 220 million years to circle around once. This time is termed a cosmic year. The spiral arms do not move around as a solid mass. All the stars within them move separately, and the ones nearer the middle complete one orbit in less time than those further out. This means that a star does not stay in the same spiral arm — it will move slowly across one arm, then faster across the space between the arms, slowing up again when it reaches the next arm. The space between the spiral arms is not empty, but the arms are where the stars and nebulae are concentrated.

THE MIDDLE OF OUR GALAXY

Astronomers cannot see to the middle of the Galaxy because it is completely hidden by thick dust. However, satellite telescopes, which use x-rays, infra-red and ultra-violet radiation, can peer through this dust to get a glimpse of the middle.

What they see is a huge cluster of stars. These are mainly cool red giant stars, much closer together than the stars in the spiral arms. Inside the cluster of stars, even closer to the middle, is a ring of gas and dust circling around the central point, with streamers of gas reaching inward. The ring of gas surrounds a clearer area with some large hot stars. No-one knows exactly what is right

Looking toward the middle of the Galaxy, all we see are masses of stars and dark dust clouds.

in the middle of our Galaxy, though astronomers know that there is something giving out radio waves, because radio telescopes pick up signals from the central point. It could be a very tight cluster of stars. On the other hand, many astronomers think that it may be a huge black hole.

THE MILKY WAY

We cannot see the spiral shape of our Galaxy because the Sun and, of course, the Earth are in one of the spiral arms. From our position inside, all we can see of our own Galaxy is a faint luminous band across the sky that we call the Milky Way. A telescope shows that it is really millions of distant stars. These are all stars in the spiral arms. We cannot see very far through the disk before our view is blocked by dust. The middle of the Galaxy is toward the constellation Sagittarius, where the Milky Way is brightest. Looking in that direction we see stars that are in the spiral arms between us and the middle of the Galaxy. Looking in the opposite direction, away from Sagittarius, we are looking out toward the edge of the Galaxy, at stars in the outer parts of the spiral arms.

Although we cannot see what our Galaxy really looks like from the outside, astronomers can see other galaxies outside the Milky Way. Among these are spiral galaxies, some seen from above, which give astronomers a good idea of what our Galaxy might look like.

This is what our Galaxy might look like if we were to travel far outside it in a spaceship. The yellow spot marks where our Solar System would be, though you would not really be able to see it among all the other stars.

4
DISTANT GALAXIES

It is almost impossible for us to imagine our own Galaxy with its thousands of billions of stars. Yet when astronomers look beyond our Galaxy they can see that it is not the only one; there are countless galaxies. They are not all like our Galaxy – they have different shapes and different sizes. Some galaxies throw out jets of gas far into space at enormous speeds. Even the smallest ones contain millions of stars while the largest ones contain thousands of billions. Astronomers do not know exactly how many galaxies there are but their best guess is about one hundred billion. These galaxies are not spread evenly through space, but cling together in clusters which then group into superclusters.

Many galaxies are shaped like ours with a mass of stars in the middle surrounded by a flat, swirling, spiral of stars.

FINDING GALAXIES

When astronomers began to study the sky with telescopes, they soon realized that there were fuzzy patches between the stars. They called these fuzzy patches "nebulae," which means clouds. Astronomers who were watching for comets sometimes mistook nebulae for comets, so to avoid this confusion they made lists, called catalogs, of all the nebulae they found.

A French astronomer and comet-hunter, Charles Messier, made one of the first of these catalogs over 200 years ago. He produced a list of 103 nebulae in 1781, and many of them are still called by their Messier catalog number today. Many thousands more have been found since as larger telescopes were built.

When astronomers looked more closely at the nebulae they found that some were star clusters and others were glowing gas clouds. However, the exact nature of thousands of the nebulae remained unexplained until the

The Small Magellanic Cloud contains mostly young blue stars.

1920s when Edwin Hubble discovered that some of them were actually other galaxies like our own but very distant.

Astronomers now think that there are about a 100 billion galaxies in the universe, but we do not know how many exactly. Each of these galaxies contains millions or billions or even thousands of billions of stars.

The Large Magellanic Cloud, our nearest galaxy, may have a slightly spiral shape. The two Magellanic Clouds are near enough to pull our Galaxy slightly out of shape.

NEARBY GALAXIES

Not all the galaxies are very far away. Our own Galaxy has two companion galaxies, which orbit around it. They are called the Large Magellanic Cloud and the Small Magellanic Cloud. They are named for the Portuguese explorer Ferdinand Magellan, whose ship was the first to sail right around the world between 1519 and 1522. His sailors reported what looked like "two clouds of mist" near the Milky Way in the southern sky — you can only see them from the Earth's southern hemisphere. The Large Magellanic Cloud is about a quarter of the size of our Galaxy, and the smaller one is only one-sixth. They are so close that astronomers have found a stream of gas linking them to our Milky Way Galaxy.

Both the Magellanic Clouds contain many bright young stars. In the Large Magellanic Cloud there is a huge glowing cloud called the Tarantula Nebula where stars are being born. In 1987 a massive star exploded in the Large Magellanic Cloud, near the Tarantula Nebula. It was very exciting for astronomers because it was the nearest and brightest supernova to be seen since 1604. It was bright enough to be seen without a telescope and lasted for many days.

MANY DIFFERENT GALAXIES

Just like the stars, the galaxies are not all the same. Photographs of the distant galaxies show many different sizes and many different shapes, although there are three main types of galaxy. About a third of all galaxies are spiral galaxies like our own Galaxy. About half are termed elliptical galaxies and these can be round like a basketball or more like a football. Galaxies of the third type do not have a definite shape and are termed "irregular" galaxies. Also, there are a few galaxies that astronomers term "peculiar" galaxies because they have different shapes that do not fit into one of the three groups.

The Tarantula Nebula is not in our Galaxy. It is a huge mass of glowing gas and stars in the Large Magellanic Cloud.

SPIRAL GALAXIES

Spiral galaxies have a central bulge of closely packed stars and arms spiralling outward in a flat disk. The stars in the middle are mainly old red stars. Further out, in the spiral arms, there are both young and old stars which are spread further apart than the stars in the bulge. The spiral arms also contain a lot of dust and glowing clouds of gas, where new stars are born.

About a third of all spiral galaxies have a bar across the middle instead of a central bulge. These are termed barred spirals. The arms curl out from the ends of the bar.

No two galaxies are the same. In some, the arms are curled around tightly, almost into a ball shape. Other galaxies have very loosely curled arms so that the spiral shape is difficult to see. Our Galaxy is in between these kinds and has a definite spiral shape. The smallest spiral galaxies have about 1 billion stars but the largest may have as many as 1,000 billion stars. The Milky Way Galaxy is one of the largest.

A spiral galaxy looked at from above. See how the arms curl around the bright centre.

ELLIPTICAL GALAXIES

These are oval-shaped collections of older stars, without any spiral arms. Some are round like a basketball while others can be shaped like footballs. There are some that are shaped like a lens, and these are termed "lenticular" galaxies.

Elliptical galaxies do not have any of the young stars and glowing gas clouds that are found in the arms of spiral galaxies. There is also less gas and dust between the stars.

This giant ball of old, red, stars is one of the largest elliptical galaxies. It probably contains over a 1,000 billion stars.

The two arms of this barred spiral galaxy start at the ends of a bar across the middle of the galaxy.

EXPLODING GALAXIES?

Astronomers used to think that everything was peaceful in the distant galaxies, with only a rare supernova explosion to disturb things. However, when radio telescopes were built in the 1940s and 1950s they discovered that some galaxies gave out very strong radio waves — in fact, about one in every 100 galaxies is a radio galaxy.

Detailed "pictures" made by modern radio telescopes show a narrow gas jet coming from near the middle of a radio galaxy. The jet stretches out into space far beyond the edge of the galaxy itself — some jets are millions of light years long. The radio waves seem to come from the streams of gas particles that are flung out from the galaxy's core at incredibly high speeds. Something inside these galaxies must be producing huge amounts of energy — much more energy than ordinary stars can make.

The Sombrero is a spiral galaxy seen from the side. The dark strip is dust in the spiral arms.

BLACK HOLE POWER

At first astronomers thought that the gas jets were caused by huge explosions at the middle of the galaxies. The most likely explanation now seems to be that they are thrown out by a black hole. It would have to be a much bigger black hole than one left after a supernova explosion. This kind is termed a supermassive black hole.

Recall that nothing can escape from a black hole, but anything nearby, like gas or even a star, is pulled toward it and becomes part of a disk surrounding it. The gas in the disk is pulled inward by gravity and spirals toward the black hole like water going down a drain. Near the middle some of the gas is thrown outward with enormous force. If the swirling disk is very thick, the gas cannot escape through it. Then it is channeled into two narrow jets racing away from the middle of the galaxy in opposite directions.

Even a supermassive black hole can only produce energy and throw out gas jets like this if there is enough gas to make a disk around it. Eventually all the available gas may be swallowed up. With nothing left to feed on, the black hole cannot give out light or radio waves or anything to show us that it is there. It may be that there is a "sleeping" black hole at the heart of most galaxies, even our own Milky Way. These would remain dormant black holes unless they are supplied with some more gas to swallow up.

QUASARS

When the first quasars (quasi-stellar radio objects) were discovered in 1960 astronomers were very puzzled. The quasars looked like stars, but unlike ordinary stars they gave out strong radio waves. What is more, although they looked like nearby stars, they were in fact very far away indeed, further away than the galaxies. They were the most distant objects that had ever been found.

The fact that they could be seen at these distances meant that they must be very bright, much brighter than the brightest galaxies. They also seemed to be extremely small compared with a galaxy. Quasars were giving out about 100 times as much energy as the whole of our Galaxy from a region about the size of the Solar System.

Where could all this energy be coming from? The most reasonable explanation is — again — a supermassive black hole inside the quasar. It seems that quasars are just like the radio galaxies except that they are much more powerful. Astronomers think that quasars may be newly formed, very young galaxies. All galaxies may have been like quasars when they were young, before they settled down to a quieter life as ordinary galaxies like ours.

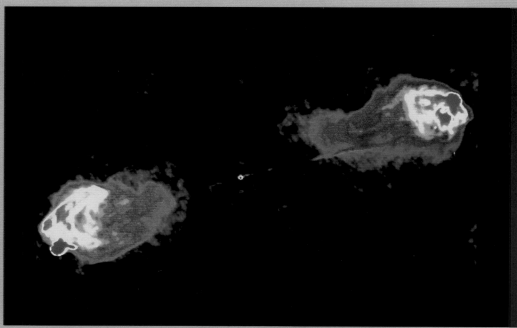

The bright colors in this radio picture show up huge areas which are giving out radio waves on either side of a galaxy. You cannot see the galaxy itself but the small dot in the middle shows where its center is. Two invisible jets of gas shoot out in opposite directions from the galaxy to these colored radio lobes.

Gas swirling in toward a supermassive black hole in the middle of a galaxy. Near the middle a narrow jet of gas streams outward.

COLLIDING GALAXIES

Among the spiral and elliptical galaxies there are some "peculiar" galaxies which have very strange shapes. Some look like double galaxies linked by a rope or a bridge. Others seem to have long tails or are surrounded by a bright ring — these are galaxies that have collided with each other. There is no bump because galaxies are not solid. What happens is that the gas and dust in a galaxy is pulled out into strange shapes by another galaxy that has come too close. One galaxy can pass right through another, causing a ripple effect in the other galaxy, like a pebble being dropped into a pond. This may cause new stars to form in a ring of glowing gas clouds and bright young stars.

CANNIBAL GALAXIES

Galaxies can behave like cannibals. Larger galaxies can pull stars away from smaller galaxies if they come too close. These large galaxies may even swallow up smaller ones. For example, there are some giant elliptical galaxies that seem to have two cores. They may have grown to this huge size by swallowing up smaller galaxies.

These elliptical and spiral galaxies belong to the nearest large cluster of galaxies called the Virgo Cluster.

THE LOCAL GROUP OF GALAXIES

Galaxies are not spread evenly through space but gather together in groups. Our Galaxy is one of a group of at least 26 called the Local Group. It is difficult to be sure exactly how many galaxies there are in the group because most of them are very small and difficult to see, especially if they are on the far side of our Galaxy. The Milky Way is the second biggest in the Local Group. The only bigger one is another spiral galaxy, called the Andromeda Galaxy. There is one other spiral, the Triangulum Galaxy, and all

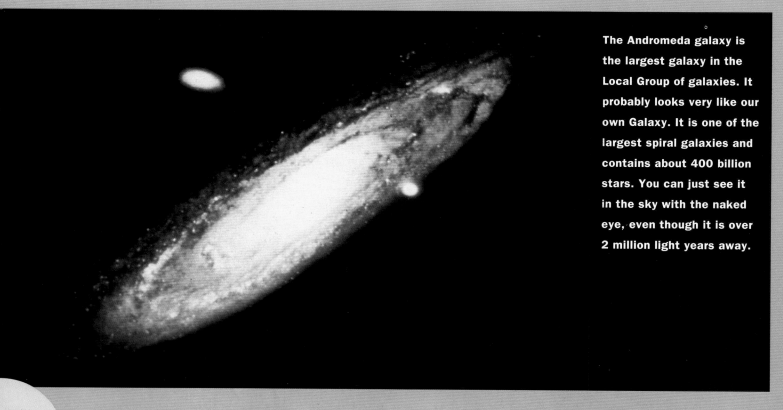

The Andromeda galaxy is the largest galaxy in the Local Group of galaxies. It probably looks very like our own Galaxy. It is one of the largest spiral galaxies and contains about 400 billion stars. You can just see it in the sky with the naked eye, even though it is over 2 million light years away.

Two galaxies have collided here, producing two long streamers of stars.

CLUSTERS OF GALAXIES

The Local Group is only a small group. Looking further afield, there are huge clusters containing thousands of galaxies. The nearest of these is the Virgo cluster which contains over 3,000 galaxies of all kinds; large spiral and elliptical, and many dwarf ones close to the larger ones. The biggest galaxy in the cluster is a giant elliptical galaxy called M87.

Even though it contains thousands of galaxies, the Virgo cluster is still small compared to others. Galaxies are held together in clusters by the pull of gravity. In the large clusters the galaxies near the middle are closer together — this is where collisions are likely to happen, and where giant elliptical galaxies are often found. These could be cannibal galaxies.

the rest are small or dwarf galaxies. Their shapes are either elliptical or irregular and most of them contain only a few million stars. These dwarf galaxies cluster in two groups around the two largest spiral galaxies.

The Milky Way, a spiral galaxy, is on the left surrounded by a group of small dwarf galaxies. The Andromeda and Triangulum spiral galaxies are in another group together with several dwarf galaxies. These two groups and a few other smaller galaxies make up the Local Group which is part of the Local Super Cluster which has Virgo at its centre.

5

THE UNIVERSE

So far we have looked at the Sun and its family of planets, beyond the Solar System to the other stars and nebulae in the Milky Way, and even further to billions of other galaxies. All of these are part of the universe. In fact, the universe consists of absolutely everything from the tiniest atomic particle to enormous superclusters of galaxies. The furthest things that astronomers can see in the universe are quasars and some of these are over 10 billion light years away. The Hubble Space Telescope is designed to probe further than ever before and discover more about the universe.

The Big Bang.

LOOKING BACK IN TIME

When we look out into space we are looking back in time. This is because light travels through space at a fixed speed of about 186,000 miles (300,000 km) every second. Although this is incredibly fast, distances in space are so enormous that the light from a distant star or galaxy takes a long time to reach us. Light takes over four years to reach Earth from the nearest star, Proxima Centauri, so we see Proxima Centauri as it was when that light left it more than four years ago, not as it is now.

We do not see anything in space as it actually is now. The further away a star is, the longer it takes for its light to reach us. So as we look far out into space we are also looking back toward earlier times in the history of the universe.

The universe has changed during its history. The most distant things that astronomers can see are quasars, which are all very far away. This probably means that when the universe was very young there were many more quasars than there are today.

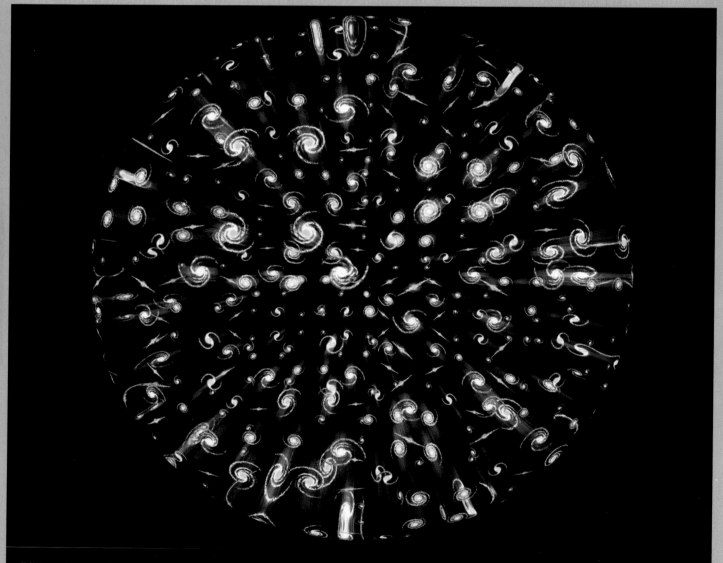

Billions of years ago, the galaxies were all racing away from each other at very high speeds, faster than they are now. They were also much closer together than they are today.

The Big Bang is the name that astronomers have given to the explosion which started the universe expanding. Astronomers cannot explain exactly what happened in the Big Bang, or why, but they think that, at first, the universe was extremely hot. The Big Bang created a fireball and everything started to move apart at very high speeds. There were no stars, planets or galaxies to start with. As the universe expanded, it gradually cooled down, and galaxies formed. The galaxies continued to race away from each other while stars were forming in them, making the universe that we live in now. Astronomers can still see the distant galaxies moving apart, but the expansion is slower now.

EXPANDING UNIVERSE

Not long after Edwin Hubble had discovered that galaxies were very far away, he made another surprising discovery. He found that all the galaxies, apart from a few nearby ones, seemed to be moving away from us. Not only that, but the more distant galaxies were moving away faster than the nearer ones. This could only mean that the whole universe is expanding — every galaxy is moving away from every other galaxy. Imagine a balloon with spots painted on it. When you blow the balloon up, all the spots get further apart. This is what is happening to the galaxies.

THE BIG BANG

What happened to make the universe start expanding in the first place? Astronomers think that there must have been a huge explosion that they call the Big Bang, and that this happened between 10 and 20 billion years ago. Scientists estimate the age of the universe by looking at the rate at which it is expanding now. They cannot measure this very accurately but they hope that the Hubble telescope will supply better information. Astronomers estimate the age of our Galaxy by looking at globular clusters which contain the oldest stars in the Galaxy.

Astronomers can tell that the universe is expanding by studying the light coming from the galaxies. If a galaxy is moving away from us, then its light will be stretched out as it travels through space. It appears redder than usual, and this is called "red shift." The red shift is larger when the galaxy is moving away more quickly.

YOUNG GALAXIES

At first there was just gas in the universe. Then, when the universe was still young, probably only about one to two billion years old, the galaxies started to form. Astronomers do not know exactly when or how this happened. It may be that gravity pulled the gas together into enormous clouds where stars began to form. Eventually they became the huge families of stars that we now see as galaxies.

BACKGROUND RADIATION

How do astronomers know about the Big Bang? Their ideas can be tested to see if they agree with what we see today. If the universe began as an incredibly hot fireball, and gradually cooled as it expanded, the remains of the fireball should still be around now — showing up as radiation coming from space.

This radiation has been found and is called the Cosmic Background Radiation. It was actually found by accident. In 1963, U.S. scientists Arno Penzias and Robert Wilson were using a special receiver at a telephone laboratory and found some interference that they could not get rid of. Whichever way they pointed the receiver they discovered exactly the same interference. This could only be the Cosmic Background Radiation. Measurements by the COBE (Cosmic Background Explorer) satellite have shown that the universe has cooled to a temperature of just less than −454 °F (−270 °C). This supports the Big Bang theory.

THE FUTURE OF THE UNIVERSE

Will the universe continue to expand or will something happen to stop it? Nobody knows the answer to this question. If the universe goes on expanding, the galaxies will continue to get further and further away from each other. The gas and dust that make all the stars in the galaxies will eventually be used up and this will mean

If the universe stops expanding, the galaxies might end up all squashed together in the "Big Crunch."

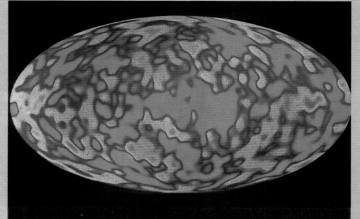

This **COBE** satellite picture of the whole sky shows tiny differences in the Cosmic Background Radiation — the pink and red parts are slightly warmer than the rest.

that there will be no more new stars. As the existing stars eventually die the galaxies will grow dark and cold.

Alternatively, the universe might stop expanding and start collapsing instead. Then the galaxies will move toward each other, getting closer and closer together until everything in the universe is squashed together again, as it was at the time of the Big Bang. This is sometimes called the Big Crunch. If this happens, everything might disappear into a giant supermassive black hole.

Some scientists have suggested that another Big Bang could start the universe expanding all over again. This

Far away, across the universe, there may be planets where the only living things are like moss or algae clinging to the rocks.

DARK MATTER

The fate of the universe depends on what it contains. The galaxies will stop flying apart if the pull of gravity between them is strong enough. The pull of gravity will be strong enough if the galaxies contain enough material including gas, dust, stars, and anything else. Astronomers can see the stars and nebulae and they know that there are not enough of these to stop the universe expanding. But is there anything else? If there is, it cannot be seen, so astronomers call it "dark matter."

This "dark matter" could be black holes, or very dim brown dwarf stars, or even some kind of particle that scientists do not know about yet. Whatever it is, there would have to be a lot of it to stop the universe expanding. There would have to be about four times as much dark matter as there is in bright objects like stars.

LIFE IN THE SOLAR SYSTEM

Humans have not yet explored very far into the universe. We have only traveled as far as the Moon and found no life of any kind there. We have sent exploring spacecraft to visit all the planets except Pluto and none of these has shown any signs of life. The planet which is most like Earth is Mars and the Viking spacecraft that landed there carried out special experiments to look for life. They scooped up Martian soil and tested it, but the results did not show any of the expected signs of life.

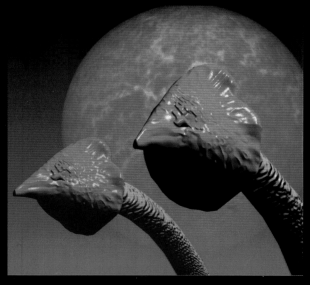

Future space explorers may meet intelligent creatures in other worlds that are very different from us.

PLANETS LIKE EARTH

Life as we know it would need a planet like the Earth on which to live. Every living thing on Earth needs water to survive, so the temperature on the planet would have to be warm enough for water to exist as a liquid — which means that it would have to be between 32 °F (0 °C) and 212 °F (100 °C). The planet would also need an atmosphere. This would help to protect any life on its surface from the damaging radiation from the Sun.

Of course, life elsewhere in the universe might be quite different from the life we know on Earth and so need a completely different kind of environment.

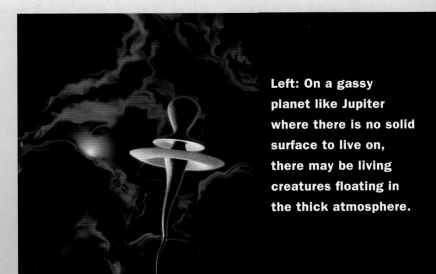

Left: On a gassy planet like Jupiter where there is no solid surface to live on, there may be living creatures floating in the thick atmosphere.

A strange city on a distant planet seen from an Earth spaceship.

85

SENDING MESSAGES INTO SPACE

Each of the two Pioneer spacecraft is carrying a metal plate away from the Solar System. The plates show a man and a woman, with a diagram of the Sun and planets along the bottom.

We have already started sending messages out toward the stars. The best way that we know of sending messages through space is by using radio waves. We have been doing this without intending to since the first radio programmes were broadcast about 70 years ago. Radio waves travel at the same speed as light, so the first ones have only traveled about 70 light years from the Earth. This is a very small hop, even compared with the distance to the middle of our own Galaxy, 30,000 light years away. There is not much chance that the radio waves have reached other intelligent beings yet.

The first deliberate attempt to try and make contact with other intelligent life was made in 1974. It was a coded message containing information about the Solar System and life on Earth. The world's largest radio telescope at Arecibo in Puerto Rico was used to send it, and it was aimed toward a globular cluster called M13 in the constellation of Hercules. There are several hundred thousand stars in that particular cluster so there is a fairly good chance of finding some planets there. The only

In 1974 the Arecibo radio telescope sent a radio message to any intelligent life-forms that might be listening out in space. As yet, there has not been any reply.

The Voyager space probes carry a long-playing disk with pictures showing how to play the sounds on it.

trouble is that it is about 25,000 light years away, so the message will take 25,000 years to get there. And if there is an answer from intelligent life there, it will get back to Earth in about 50,000 years' time!

There are four spacecraft heading out of the Solar System and they all carry messages in case they encounter life elsewhere. The two Pioneer spacecraft each have a plaque showing pictures of a man and a woman and a diagram of the Solar System. The two Voyager probes carry long-playing records that contain sounds of Earth and greetings in many different languages. But unfortunately it is very unlikely that these spacecraft and their messages will ever meet any other intelligent life.

IS THERE ANYBODY OUT THERE?

Many scientists believe that we have more chance of making contact with other intelligent life if we listen for messages from outer space ourselves. They have set up projects called SETI (Search for Extraterrestrial Intelligence). This uses radio telescopes to pick up radio signals from space. These are then carefully analyzed to see if there is anything that could be a message for us from outer space. They have not found anything yet.

UFOS

Some people think that we have already had visitors from outer space. There are many reports of UFOs (unidentified flying objects), which are strange objects seen in the sky. Most of them can be explained as, for instance, a strangely shaped cloud or a trick of the sunlight. There have been a few that are unexplained and some people believe that these could be alien spacecraft.

However, we would need much better evidence than these sightings before we could even begin to think that visitors have been anywhere near our planet Earth. But the possibility that there might be other life-forms in space continues to fascinate us all.

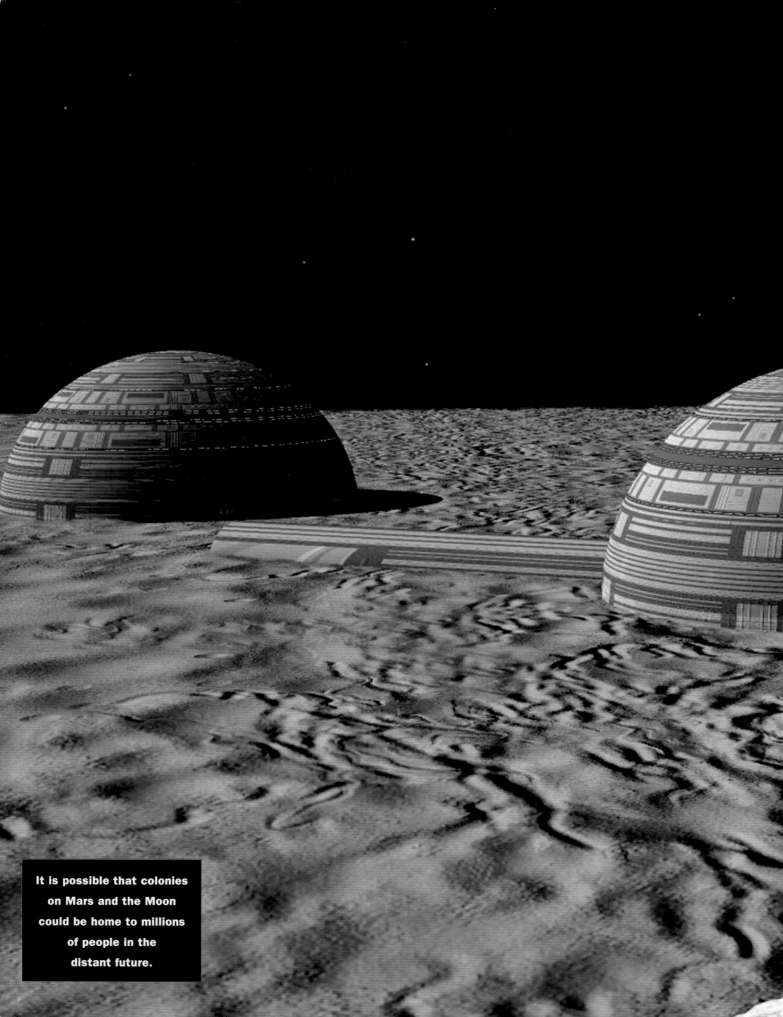

It is possible that colonies on Mars and the Moon could be home to millions of people in the distant future.

OUR FUTURE IN SPACE

What future is there for humans in space? Is it possible that in the next century people may have permanent homes in space, in colonies on the Moon or Mars, or in huge orbiting space cities? These independent "island communities," built with materials mined on the Moon or asteroids, will grow their own food and recycle their air and water. They could be used to launch the first starships to explore the distant stars beyond our Solar System.

EXPLORING SPACE

The whole of the universe is out there waiting to be explored. However, there are many problems, the first of which is just getting off the Earth and into space.

Everything on the Earth is held down by the pull of the Earth's gravity. Without this we would all float away into space. To escape from this pull of gravity, you have to travel very fast. It is like throwing a ball up in the air — the harder you throw it, the higher it goes. If you could throw it hard and fast enough it would escape right out of the Earth's atmosphere. But it would need to travel at a speed of 25,000 miles (40,000km) per hour — 20 times faster than Concorde — to escape from the Earth completely.

The huge Soyuz rocket launches the Russian cosmonauts into space for their visits to the Mir space station.

ROCKETS INTO SPACE

Satellites and spacecraft are launched into space by powerful rockets that can give them the speed they need. Satellites do not escape completely from the pull of gravity, though. They stay in orbit round the Earth, which means that they need to travel at "only" 17,000 miles (28,000km) per hour!

To reach these speeds rockets have several parts, termed stages, stacked on top of each other. Each one of these stages has its own motor and fuel tanks. The lowest, or first-stage, engine fires first, pushing the rocket upward faster and faster. When all its fuel is used up, the first stage separates from the rocket and falls away, leaving the second-stage motor to fire and carry the rocket even higher and faster toward space. The last stage takes the satellite or spacecraft into space, and either puts it into orbit or sends it on its journey away from the Earth.

Aircraft and rocket fuels will not burn without oxygen. There is plenty of oxygen in the Earth's atmosphere so aircraft engines use this to burn their fuel. There is no oxygen in space, so rockets carry their own supply. In some rockets, the fuel and oxygen are mixed together in a solid lump which burns inside the rocket. Other rockets use liquid fuels in two tanks, one containing fuel and the other containing an oxygen supply. These liquids are mixed in the engine, where they burn to produce hot gases, which escape out of a nozzle at the end of the rocket.

These gases, rushing out, push the rocket forward at ever-increasing speeds. The same thing happens if you blow up a balloon and let it go — the air rushes out and sends the balloon shooting off in the opposite direction.

The Ariane rocket, with its three stages and extra booster rockets, carries satellites into orbit around the Earth.

APOLLO – ROCKET TO THE MOON

One of the largest rockets ever built was the Saturn V rocket that sent the Apollo astronauts on their historic journey to the Moon in 1969. This giant rocket was 363 feet (111m) tall and weighed 3,000 tons at launch. It had three stages and the first stage alone had five engines which were as powerful as 160 jumbo jet engines. Perched on top of this monster was a tiny spacecraft, consisting of a Command Module with three astronauts on board, a Service Module which carried the main equipment, and the Lunar Module — the part that would carry two of the astronauts to the surface of the Moon and back to the Command Module. The first astronauts to land on the Moon were launched on July 16th, 1969.

JOURNEY TO THE MOON

The Saturn V rocket carried the spacecraft with its three passengers into orbit round the Earth, then gave it an extra boost to break free from the pull of Earth's gravity and send it on its way toward the Moon. The Command and Service Module, known as Columbia, joined up with the Lunar Module, known as the Eagle (which would land on the Moon) and they continued the journey together. It took about three days to get to the Moon. Once there the spacecraft went into orbit round the Moon.

One of the astronauts, Michael Collins, stayed in the Command and Service Module orbiting the Moon. The other two astronauts climbed into the Lunar Module, which landed on the surface of the Moon on July 20th, 1969.

The next day, July 21st, Neil Armstrong, wearing his Apollo spacesuit, climbed down the ladder from the Lunar Module to put the first human foot on the Moon. He was

LEFT: Edwin Aldrin jumps down to become the second man to set foot on the Moon.
BELOW: The Apollo 12 Lunar Module flies above the Moon's craters on its way to a landing.
BOTTOM: Jim Irwin gets the first Moon Buggy ready for an exploring trip.

soon followed out by Edwin (Buzz) Aldrin, and they stayed out on the surface for nearly three hours. They found that walking was difficult in their bulky spacesuits so they had to bounce along the surface instead. They collected 46lb (21kg) of Moon rock to take back to Earth and set up experiments to leave there, before climbing back into the Lunar Module, which lifted the two astronauts back up to dock with Columbia. Aldrin and Armstrong went back into the Command and Service Module, leaving the Lunar

Module behind, and started on the return journey back to Earth. Three days later the Command Module parachuted through the Earth's atmosphere to splash down in the sea where a ship was waiting to pick it up together with the astronauts.

The first astronauts on the Moon were kept in isolation when they returned to Earth in case they had brought back any unknown infections. But this turned out to be unnecessary. Nothing living has ever been found on the Moon.

WEIGHTLESSNESS

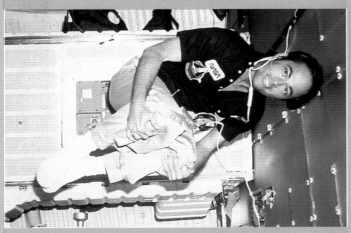

There is one really big difference between life on Earth and life on board a space station or the Space Shuttle orbiting the Earth — weightlessness, which means that everything in space appears to float. If you are orbiting the Earth in a spacecraft, the Earth's pull of gravity keeps both you and the spacecraft falling around the Earth in a great circular orbit. However, there is nothing to pull you down to the "floor" of the spacecraft, in the way that gravity pulls you down to the ground when you are on Earth.

So, you appear to float inside the spacecraft, along with everything else. In fact, the spacecraft does not have a floor or a ceiling because there is no "up" or "down" as we understand it on Earth. Many astronauts suffer from space sickness when they are first in space, before they get used to it. They find that it helps to decide which way is "up," and to call one wall of the spacecraft the "floor" and another the "ceiling."

Aldrin is well protected by his tough spacesuit on the first Apollo trip to the Moon.

One of the astronauts is firmly fixed to the Space Shuttle's special arm as they capture a satellite from its orbit around the Earth. The satellite can be repaired in the Shuttle or returned to Earth. You can see the Sun shining on the Earth and the darkness of space in the background.

Two huge booster rockets and the Shuttle's three rocket engines provide the power and speed required to send the Space Shuttle Atlantis into space. It will orbit the Earth at a height of about 155 miles (250km) and at a speed of 17,400 miles (28,000km) per hour.

THE SPACE SHUTTLE

Rockets like Saturn V are very expensive to build, and the whole thing is destroyed when it is launched so it can only be used once.

As far as possible, the Space Shuttle was designed to be reusable. The Shuttle orbiter itself looks rather like a plane with wings and a tail, but it has rocket engines. The fuel for these engines is in a huge separate tank which is attached to the Shuttle during the launch. As well as its own rocket engines, two large booster rockets help to lift the Shuttle off the ground and launch it into space.

About two minutes after launch, when the booster rockets have used up all their fuel, they separate from the Shuttle and parachute down to land in the sea. They are recovered and used again for another Shuttle launch. The fuel tank is the only part that is not used again. It goes into space before separating from the Shuttle, and is burnt up as it falls back into the atmosphere.

Once in space, the Shuttle orbits the Earth with its crew of astronauts and its cargo. The astronauts can launch new satellites into space from the Shuttle's cargo bay or recapture damaged satellites and repair them before putting them back into orbit. The astronauts stay in space for at least a week before the Shuttle re-enters the atmosphere and glides down to Earth. It lands on a runway like an airplane, except that it does not use engines, so it is more like a giant glider. A few weeks later it is ready for another trip into space.

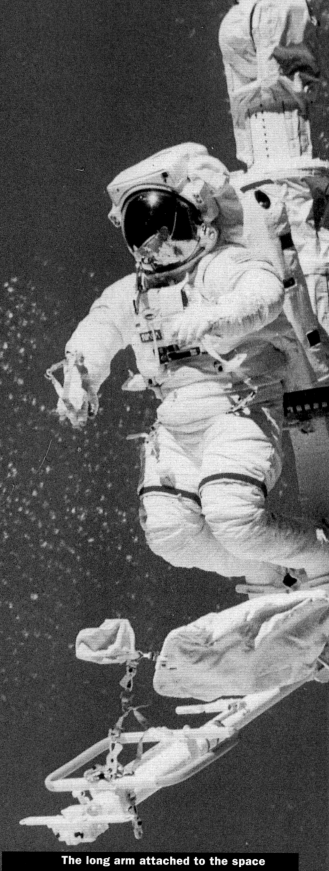

SPACESUITS

Most of the time astronauts stay in the safety of their spacecraft. If they want to go out into space to repair a satellite or carry out some repairs to the space-craft, they must wear a spacesuit.

This spacesuit is a personal life support system — like a space station in miniature. It provides air to breathe and protects the astronaut's body from all the dangers of space. Without a spacesuit a human in space would die because gas would bubble out of the blood as though it were boiling. This does not happen to us on Earth because of the pressure of the Earth's atmosphere on the body, but in space the spacesuit must provide this pressure. It does this by means of a body-shaped balloon which is full of air that presses all over the body.

Underneath this, the astronaut wears a cooling suit next to the skin. Although it is very cold in space, it would get very hot sealed inside a spacesuit if body heat was not taken away. The cooling suit has a network of tubes, through which water circulates to carry heat away from the skin. The outer part of the spacesuit is made of many layers of tough material to protect the astronaut from radiation and from tiny dust particles. These fly through space fast enough to

The shiny visor on the spacesuit helmet protects the Shuttle astronaut's eyes from the Sun's light. Astronauts can also wear a jet-propelled backpack that lets them turn or move freely in any direction.

The long arm attached to the space Shuttle provides a platform for astronauts working outside and stops them from floating away from the Shuttle.

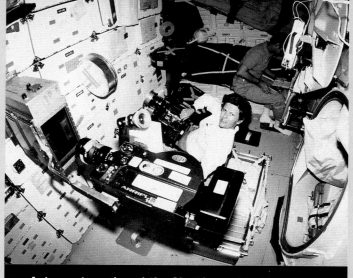

Astronauts on board the Shuttle are kept busy with many experiments and jobs to do in space.

SLEEPING

In space, because of weightlessness, you do not need a bed for support when you are sleeping, but you do need to stop yourself from floating around. A sleeping bag or a blanket with straps is all astronauts need. However, spacecraft tend to be busy, noisy places so astronauts wear earplugs and masks over their eyes to help them sleep well.

EATING

All food must be brought up from Earth so a lot of it is dried to save weight. Astronauts prepare their meals by adding hot or cold water to individual containers of food and they have an oven to warm it up if necessary.

In weightless conditions food would not stay on a plate, and drinks would float out of a cup, so great care has to be taken not to let food or drink float around. If any crumbs or drops of liquid were to get into electrical equipment they could cause serious problems, even putting the astronauts' safety at risk. So the food is all in individual containers and the drinks are in squeezy packs.

The astronauts have meal trays that they can fix to a table or wall while eating, and they can use footholds or a seat belt to steady themselves. They can use a knife, fork and spoon but they must avoid sudden movements that could make the food shoot off the fork or spoon. They squeeze or suck drinks out of the packs. In space, liquids form themselves into round balls, rather like bubbles, and are not very easy to catch if they escape.

go right through a thinner suit.

The suit is connected to a backpack which carries a supply of oxygen to breathe — enough for about six or seven hours in space. The whole suit is very bulky and has special joints to help the arms move more easily. The helmet has a visor to protect the eyes from the blinding light of the Sun. Underneath the helmet the astronaut wears a cap with headphones for communicating with the other astronauts inside the space station.

KEEPING CLEAN

Weightlessness in space makes washing and keeping clean more of a problem. Water does not flow out of faucets in a stream, it simply floats around. So a current of air directs it onto your hands for washing and then sucks the dirty water away into a waste water tank.

In the same way, when an astronaut uses the bathroom in space, air currents pull the waste solids and liquids away

from the body and into waste containers. It is important to seal all the waste containers and keep everything very clean. This is because any illness would spread very quickly inside an enclosed space station.

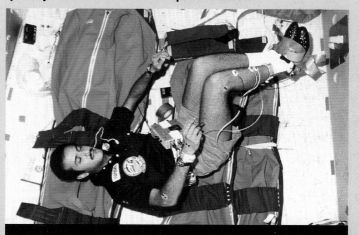

The weightlessness of space means that an astronaut's life can be literally turned upside-down.

SPACE STATIONS

Mir (Peace), the Russian space station, was the first to be built in space. In 1986 a basic module was launched, with living quarters for the crew and controls for the space station. Apart from a few months, cosmonauts (the Russian word for astronauts) have been living in it ever since. Since then, three other modules have been launched and have joined up with Mir in space, making a much larger space station. These modules have telescopes and equipment for making special, very pure crystals which can only be made properly in space.

The cosmonauts travel up to the space station and back again to Earth in a Soyuz spacecraft. This docks with the Mir space station until it is time to return to Earth. Supplies are brought from Earth in an unmanned Progress spacecraft, which carries food, water, and oxygen for astronauts to breathe and as fuel for Mir's engines.

Between December 1987 and December 1988 two cosmonauts, Vladimir Titov and Musa Manarov, spent a whole year in Mir. This is the longest time anyone has spent in space since space travel began.

Cosmonauts live and work on board the Russian space station Mir, which is now even larger than this.

The USA is planning to build a space station called Freedom, where astronauts will live and work. Space Shuttles will ferry the necessary parts and materials and they will be put together by astronauts in space. When it is built, the Shuttle will travel between the space station and Earth carrying people and supplies. The new space station could be a starting point for voyages to the Moon, or Mars, or even the other planets.

SPACE CITIES

These space stations are just the beginning. In the future, people from Earth could live their whole lives in huge cities in space, quite separate from Earth. Several designs for space cities have been suggested, but they are all very big and would be very expensive and difficult to build.

Problems caused by long-term weightlessness in space could be overcome by making the space station spin around at a constant speed, which would push everything out toward the edge of the space station. This is what happens when you swing a weight around in a circle on the end of a piece of cord. The spinning weight tries to fly outward, pulling the cord taut. If the space station were a large cylinder or ring-shaped, anyone inside would be pushed toward the outer wall, which would feel the same as gravity pulling you down to the ground on Earth. This is called artificial gravity.

Space cities would be huge, at least a mile across, and inside would be gently curving landscapes with plants and trees, just like valleys in a pleasant part of the Earth. There would be living areas with stores and apartments. Food would be grown in special areas and in others there would be factories where the people would work.

Inside a huge ring-shaped space city being built, the wall curves away into the distance. This will be the ground that people will live on.

RECYCLING TO LIVE

A space city this big could not rely on supplies being brought up from Earth as space stations do now. Everything that everybody used would have to be recycled. Water could be cleaned and used again and again. Human and animal waste could be sterilized and used as fertilizer for the plants.

Here on Earth we now reuse or recycle many materials instead of throwing them away. Objects like glass bottles can be used many times, and others, such as paper and metal cans, can be recycled after use and made into new products.

Hundreds of years from now people may live their whole lives in huge spaceships as they travel between the stars.

KEEPING FIT

Here on Earth gravity is always pulling us downward and our muscles have to work hard to hold our bodies upright. In space, without this strong pull of gravity, an astronaut's muscles become weaker and the bones thinner. The blood is not pulled down toward the feet — instead it tends to rise to the head and chest. Astronauts even grow a little taller while they are in space because they are not pulled down by gravity. So it is very important to exercise, to work the muscles that have nothing to do in space. Astronauts use an exercise bicycle or a treadmill, which they are held onto by straps. Russian cosmonauts who have stayed in space for months at a time also use a special suit. This pulls the blood back down to their legs, and it helps them prepare for the return to Earth.

Four space tugs have captured an asteroid and are towing it through space so that its materials can be used to build space colonies.

BUILDING IN SPACE

It would not be practical to build these huge cities in space with materials brought all the way up from the Earth. The powerful rockets that must be used to launch anything into space from the Earth are much too expensive. It would be a much easier and cheaper to get the materials in space itself, for example, from the Moon. Alternatively, asteroids could provide another supply of building materials. One suggestion is that a space tug could tow a small asteroid into orbit round the Earth, where its materials could be mined and used to build a space city.

A space city that was a permanent home for people in space would need to have a very thick outer wall. This would be needed to protect the people from the dangerous radiation in space. It would also have to keep the space city's air in and stop it leaking out into space. And it must be thick enough to absorb impacts from dust or small rocks flying through space without any serious damage.

POWER, LIGHT, AND HEAT

In space, near the Earth, there is no shortage of light and heat from the Sun. The natural light of the Sun would shine into the space city through windows, reflected in by huge mirrors. These could be adjusted to make it dark at "night-time."

The Sun could also provide all the power needed to run the space station. Power can be supplied by solar cells which produce electricity when sunlight shines on them — you may already have a calculator or watch that runs on the power from solar cells. Or the Sun could be used to heat water in the boilers of a space power station. This would generate electricity just like power stations on Earth.

A space city like this could provide a comfortable home for thousands or even millions of people. They could live there all their lives, with maybe an occasional vacation on the Moon or the Earth. However, space cities would be incredibly expensive to build.

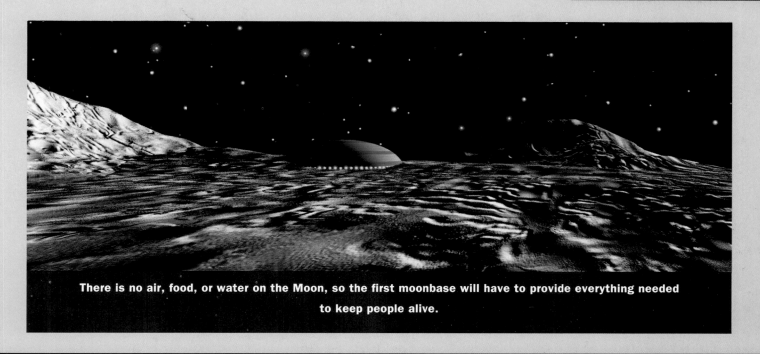

There is no air, food, or water on the Moon, so the first moonbase will have to provide everything needed to keep people alive.

Strong domes make ideal buildings for colonies on the Moon or Mars. Rover vehicles carry people and goods between the buildings and spacecraft.

THE NEW COLONIES

Instead of space cities, it would probably be easier and more practical to build colonies on the Moon or Mars, where people could live and work. Some of the problems would be the same, but there would be no need to provide artificial gravity. Although the pull of gravity is much weaker than on the Earth, people on the Moon or Mars would not be weightless. Their weight on the Moon would be one-sixth of their Earth weight and on Mars it would be about one-third of what they weighed on Earth. In fact, it would probably feel very comfortable.

Building a base would also be much simpler because the building materials could be made from rocks found on the surface of the Moon or Mars.

Like a space city, the buildings would have to be airtight because there is no air on the Moon and very little on Mars, with no oxygen for people to breathe. This means that when they went outside, on the surface, people would always have to wear spacesuits. The buildings would probably be dome-shaped or, possibly, built underground to provide extra protection against radiation.

Life inside a Martian or Lunar colony would be very like living in a space city. People would grow their own food and recycle the air and water and waste materials so that they would not need to rely on the Earth to keep them supplied. They would work at mining and producing valuable materials from the rocks, to send back to Earth or for building in space. The Moon would also be a very good place to build an observatory where astronomers could study the universe. This is because, on the Moon, there is no atmosphere to obscure the view.

The surface of Mars in the process of "terraforming" – making its atmosphere more like Earth's. The air is already thick enough for thunder clouds to form. The hills are green with the first plants grown from seed from Earth.

Air ships floating in the thin atmosphere might be a good way for explorers to travel across the surface of Mars.

A TRIP TO MARS

After the Moon, the next place for astronauts to explore is Mars. The USA and Russia have both looked at plans to send astronauts to Mars, but it would be so expensive that the latest suggestion is to send a joint expedition there.

It will not be easy. The journey to Mars and back will take over a year and the spacecraft will have to carry everything a team of astronauts needs to stay alive for all that time. It must also carry enough fuel to get there and back. It is most likely that the spacecraft would be built while in orbit round the Earth.

MARS — A HOME FOR HUMANS?

Some scientists dream that it might be possible to change the atmosphere on Mars so that eventually people would be

able to live out on the surface just as they do on Earth. This process is termed "terraforming," but it would take hundreds of thousands of years!

Firstly the surface would have to be warmed. The gases that trap the Sun's heat would be introduced into Mars's atmosphere. This would gradually warm the planet's surface and in a few hundred years some of the ice frozen in the soil and in the polar ice caps would melt. With running water in rivers and seas on the surface, simple plants could begin to grow. Very gradually, over thousands of years, the plants would convert some of the carbon dioxide gas in the atmosphere to oxygen gas — this is what happened on the Earth many millions of years ago. When there is enough oxygen, animals and humans might be able to live on Mars in the very distant future. Until then any visitors to Mars would have to live in colonies, sealed to hold in the air and warmth. Outside, on the surface, visitors would still need to wear spacesuits.

A Mars base might be built in an ancient river bed, now a dry and dusty valley. The communications tower would have a large aeriel for keeping in touch with Earth.

STARSHIPS

Mars is only a tiny step away when you have the whole of the universe to explore. Will it ever be possible to build starships that can go out and explore our Galaxy?

There is one enormous problem to be overcome and that is the vast distances a starship would have to travel. The nearest star to our Sun is over four light years away. This means that light from this star takes over four years to reach us, and nothing can travel faster than light. The speediest spacecraft that we can build today travel at least a hundred times slower than this, so they would take hundreds of years to reach even the nearest stars. For them to travel any faster, we would have to build much more efficient engines for our spacecraft.

But even if we could travel almost as fast as light, it would take 30,000 years to get to the middle of our

Huge spaceships traveling to the stars could not take off from or land on a planet. They would have to be built in space.

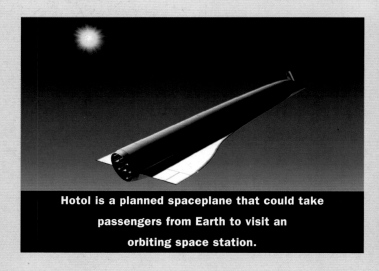

Hotol is a planned spaceplane that could take passengers from Earth to visit an orbiting space station.

Galaxy. For journeys that would last less than a lifetime, we would still be limited to a very small part of the Galaxy. It is only in science fiction that starships travel fast enough to visit different stars and planets.

One alternative would be to send huge starships, like space cities, with thousands of people aboard, traveling out into space. Because of the huge distances between stars, the astronauts who started the journey would not live long enough to see the starship reach its destination. However, their grandchildren or great-grandchildren could explore and maybe settle on a new planet far from Earth.

Spaceships do not have to be streamlined like airplanes. They can be any shape because there is no air in space to slow them down.

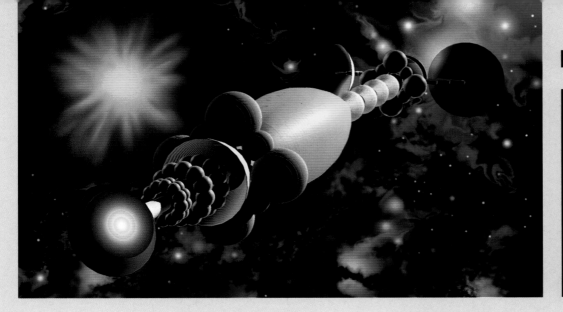

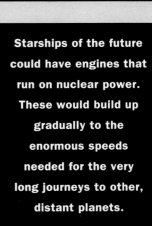

Starships of the future could have engines that run on nuclear power. These would build up gradually to the enormous speeds needed for the very long journeys to other, distant planets.

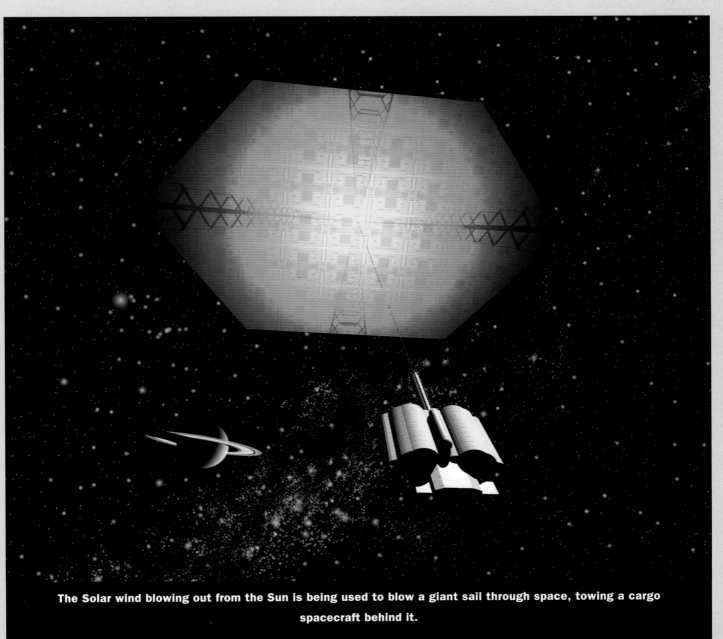

The Solar wind blowing out from the Sun is being used to blow a giant sail through space, towing a cargo spacecraft behind it.

This picture of the Milky
Way was taken from
Australia, with a special
camera lens, to show it
stretching across the
whole sky.

7

EXPLORING FROM HOME

From home you can see some of the exciting things we have talked about in the previous chapters. Start sky watching from your own yard — you do not need any special equipment. There is a lot you can see with your eyes alone. However if you have an ordinary pair of binoculars you will be able to see objects like the Moon in much more detail.

THE NIGHT SKY

When you go out to start watching the night sky remember to wear plenty of warm clothes. Very clear nights are best for seeing the stars, but they also tend to be very cold. In the winter you may even need a blanket or a sleeping bag to keep your legs warm. Get into a comfortable position for looking up at the sky; a deck chair is good for this. If you are using binoculars try to support them, so that you get a steady view through them.

One of the biggest problems is getting away from the stray light from house and street lights. However, even in well lit towns and cities, you will still be able to see the brighter stars and planets. If you can get out into the country where there are no streetlights you will be amazed at how many more stars you can see. Unless you particularly want to study the Moon, star-watching is best done on a night when there is no moonlight to overpower the much fainter light from the stars.

When you first go outside you will only see the brighter stars. However your eyes will soon adjust to the darkness and then you begin to see the fainter stars as well. It takes about half an hour to adjust completely to being in the dark. After that, avoid bright lights otherwise you will have to adjust over again. Use a red light to look at a star map – a torch covered with red transparent film will work well. Red light does not affect our eyes' ability to adapt to seeing in the dark.

MOON WATCHING

The Moon is a good place to start exploring the sky. The first thing you will notice about it are its phases. When the

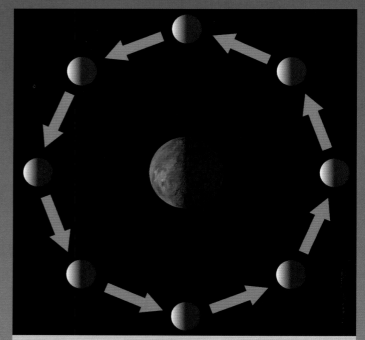

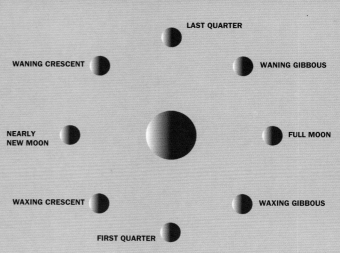

The Moon seems to change shape, from a narrow crescent when the sunlit half is facing away from us, to a full Moon when the sunlit side is facing toward us.

FIRST QUARTER

WAXING GIBBOUS

FULL MOON

WANING GIBBOUS

A SUN PROJECTOR

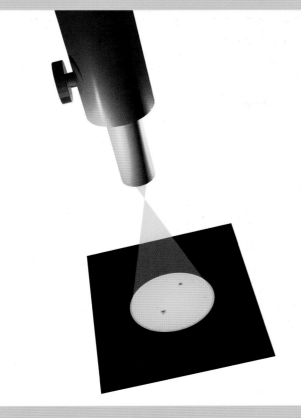

The only safe way to study the Sun is to use a telescope or a pair of binoculars to make an image (picture) of the Sun on a piece of paper. Point the telescope at the Sun by looking at its shadow, being very careful not to look at the Sun through the telescope. When the shadow is smallest the telescope will be roughly lined up with the Sun. Rest a piece of white paper under the eyepiece of the telescope and then adjust the paper and telescope until you can see a clear picture of the Sun on the paper. You may see a group of dark sunspots on the Sun. Look at them every few days to see them change position. This is because the Sun is spinning round like everything else in space, taking the sunspots with it. It takes about 27 days to spin once on its axis.

Moon is full it is in the sky all night, rising in the east at sunset and setting in the west at dawn. When the Moon is a thin crescent it is in the sky during the day and you may see it in the western evening sky near the horizon as it follows the Sun down. If you are up early you may also see the old crescent Moon in the eastern sky just before the Sun rises. These are the times when you might see the "young Moon in the old Moon's arms." As well as the bright crescent you can just see the rest of the Moon very dimly. The dark side of the Moon is lit by sunlight reflected off the Earth onto the Moon. This is termed "earthshine."

It is best to avoid a full Moon if you want to see details on the surface of the Moon. This is because the Sun is then shining directly down onto the part of the Moon's surface that is facing the Earth. So the shadows it casts on the Moon's surface are very small, making the craters difficult to see. However, you can see the dark areas that are still called "seas" even though there is no water on the Moon. The brighter areas are the Moon's highland regions.

Binoculars will enable you to see craters on the Moon. When the Moon is about half full look along the boundary between the sunlit part and the rest of the Moon. This is called the "terminator" and it is where the shadows cast by the Sun's light are longest so the mountains and crater walls show up most clearly.

> **NEVER EVER LOOK AT THE SUN THROUGH BINOCULARS OR A TELESCOPE. DO NOT EVEN LOOK DIRECTLY AT THE SUN WITH JUST YOUR EYES. ITS LIGHT IS SO BRIGHT THAT IT CAN MAKE YOU BLIND.**

LAST QUARTER

WANING CRESCENT

NEW MOON

WAXING CRESCENT

STARS AND CONSTELLATIONS

When you start looking at the stars the sky can seem very confusing, but it does not take long to recognize a few of the brightest constellations. Once you can find these, they will guide you to other constellations like signposts.

Many of these patterns were picked out and given names thousands of years ago by astronomers from ancient Greece. Some constellations look much like the shapes their names suggest. Orion the Hunter is a good example of this. Sometimes, however, you need to have a good imagination to see the picture the ancient Greeks saw in the sky. The stars in a particular constellation are not necessarily close together in space. They all lie in the same direction but some may be much further away than others.

STAR MAPS

On the star maps the brightest stars, shown by the largest dots, are named, and the main stars of each constellation are joined up by lines. (You have to imagine the lines when you are looking at the sky.) The constellation names are in bold type. One map shows the stars you can see if you live north of the equator and the other shows the southern hemisphere.

Use the map for your part of the world. You will not be able to see all the stars on your map. The stars near the middle of your map are always in the sky where you live but they can never be seen from the other half of the Earth. The stars near the edges of each map are seen in the northern hemisphere for part of the year and in the southern hemisphere for the rest of the year.

NORTHERN STARS

If you live north of the equator probably the easiest constellation to find is the Plough, also called the Dipper. The Plough is part of a larger constellation called the Great Bear or Ursa Major. Look for seven stars in the shape of a saucepan. If you look carefully at the second star from the left, called Mizar, you may be able to see that it makes a double star with another fainter star, Alcor. Telescopes will show that Mizar itself is also a double star. The two stars at the other end of the Plough are called the Pointers because

These stars and constellations can all be seen from north of the equator – can you find some of them?

The star chart (left) shows constellations including:

Cetus, (Mira), Pisois Austrinus, Aquarius, Fomalhaut, Fornax, Phoenix, Capricornus, Eridanus, Grus, Serpens, Orio, Rigel, Lepus, Hydrus, Tucana, Indus, Columba, Small Magellanic Cloud, Large Magellanic Cloud, Dorado, South Pole, Sagittarius, Canis Major, Canopus, Triang. Aust., Ara, Scorpius, Sirius, Carina, Musca, Puppis, Crux, α Centauri, Antares, β Centauri, Lupus, Centaurus, 45°, Libra, Hydra, Crater, Corvus, Spica, Virgo

LEFT: These are the brightest stars and constellations in the southern skies. The Milky Way is brighter here, and you can see the Magellanic clouds.
BELOW: The Plough at the top of the picture points down to the Pole Star, just left of center, and on to the W shape of Cassiopeia near the bottom. The Pole Star is in Ursa Minor (Little Bear) and the other constellation is called Cepheus.

they point toward Polaris, the Pole Star. This star is almost directly above the Earth's North Pole, and, unlike the other stars, it does not move across the sky as the Earth rotates.

Follow the line from the Plough past the Pole Star and you come to a constellation called Cassiopeia. It is a W or M shape that is easy to pick out. On very clear dark nights you can see the misty band of the Milky Way running right behind Cassiopeia. With a telescope or binoculars you can see some of the many billions of faint stars that make up the Milky Way. Look for the dark patches where dust clouds are hiding the light from the more distant stars.

Continuing on past Cassiopeia you come to a large square shape with a star in each corner. This is the square of Pegasus. The first star nearest to Cassiopeia is really in the constellation Andromeda. This stretches out in a line below Cassiopeia. Between them you may just be able to see a faint blur which is the spiral galaxy called the Andromeda galaxy. With binoculars it looks like a misty patch. It is over two million light years away, and is the furthest thing you can see in the sky with the naked eye.

SOUTHERN STARS

If you live south of the equator, the sights of the night sky are quite different. There is no distinct star which marks the position of the South Pole like Polaris, the Pole Star, in the northern hemisphere. One constellation that you should always be able to pick out is the Southern Cross (called Crux on the map). The Milky Way goes right behind the four stars that make the cross, and very close to them you may see a dark patch in the Milky Way. This is called the Coal Sack nebula and it is a dusty cloud in the spiral arms of our Galaxy.

Close to the Southern Cross are two bright stars, the brightest stars in the constellation of Centaurus. The furthest one from the Southern Cross is called Alpha Centauri. It is the nearest star that you can see with the naked eye, just over four light years away. It has a fainter companion called Proxima Centauri, which is the nearest star to the Sun, but you cannot see this without a telescope. Also in the constellation Centaurus, not far from the Southern Cross, is the brightest globular cluster in the sky. It is called Omega Centauri and it may contain a million stars. However it just looks like a single star unless you have very powerful binoculars.

The stars that mark the length of the Southern Cross are pointers to the South Pole. If you follow that line you come to a misty patch that is the Small Magellanic Cloud, and to one side is the brighter patch of the Large Magellanic Cloud. These are the two companion galaxies to our Milky Way Galaxy.

SEASONAL STARS

Seasonal stars are the ones that can be seen from both the northern and the southern hemisphere, but at different times of the year. Perhaps the easiest of these constellations to find is Orion which is in the northern hemisphere in winter and in southern skies for the rest of the year. You will easily spot the row of three bright stars making Orion's belt. It is surrounded by four bright stars and one of these, Betelgeuse, is distinctly red in color.

Betelgeuse is actually a red supergiant star. To see how red it is, compare it with the bright star at the opposite corner. This is Rigel, a bluish white supergiant star. Below the center of the belt is a link of faint stars which mark Orion's sword, and a closer look will show a misty patch in the sword. This is the Orion Nebula. It is a huge cloud of glowing gas where new stars are being born. Binoculars will show some of its color but nothing like the beautiful photographs taken with large telescopes.

A passing space ship might see this view of the edge of our Galaxy, with the Andromeda galaxy to the right and the Magellanic clouds on the left. The arrow shows where the Sun would be, toward the edge of our Galaxy.

A distant galaxy, called Centaurus A, which can only be seen with a very large telescope, has a dark band of dust.

Remember that if you live south of the equator Orion will appear upside-down compared with the view from the north, so you have to reverse all these directions. Follow the line of the belt stars down and to the left to find the brightest star in the sky, Sirius, or the Dog Star. Even though Sirius is often near the horizon it is so bright you can easily see it.

If you follow the line of the belt stars in the opposite direction, you will come to a red-orange star called Aldebaran. This is another red giant. Close to it is a bright cluster called the Haydes. A little further along this line takes you to a misty patch which is actually a brilliant cluster of young bluish stars. These are called the Pleiades, or the Seven Sisters, though only six of them are bright enough to see with the naked eye. It is beautiful seen through binoculars when many more stars become visible.

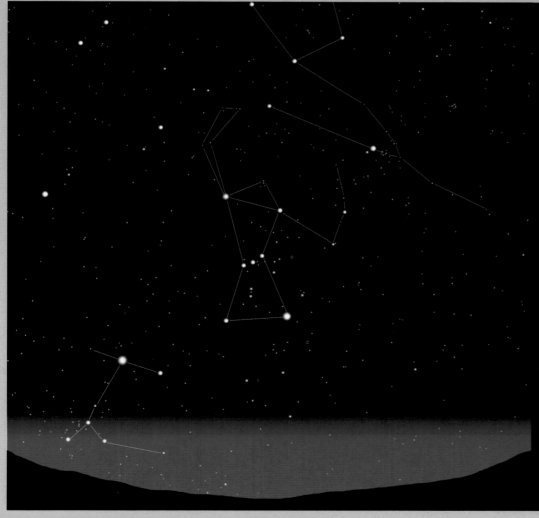

You can easily see the constellation Orion, in the middle of this picture, with its row of three bright stars surrounded by a rectangle of four stars – Betelgeuse at the top left and Rigel at the lower right. Sirius is the very bright star to the left of Orion. On the opposite side of Orion is another red giant, Aldebaran, and further toward the top right-hand corner of the picture is a cluster of stars called the Seven Sisters (Pleiades).

LOOKING FOR PLANETS

The planets are more difficult to find because they change position against the background of the stars. Planets look rather like stars in the sky except they do not twinkle as much. This is because they are much nearer to us than the stars so they seem larger and our turbulent atmosphere has less effect on their light. To find out where to look for them, use the monthly star maps given in some newspapers or buy an annual sky guide.

Mercury is very difficult to spot because it is always close to the Sun. It is never in the sky when the sky is really dark, only in twilight, just after sunset, or just before dawn, and it is always very near the horizon.

Venus, on the other hand, is the easiest planet to spot, because when it is visible it is the brightest object in the night sky apart from the Moon. It is often seen as the first bright "star" to appear in the evening sky, in the west soon after sunset. At other times it can be the last "star" to disappear from the eastern morning sky. Because of this it is often called the "evening star" or the "morning star."

Mars can be picked out because of its red color and it is often quite bright depending on how close it is to Earth in its orbit. Like all the other planets and the Moon, its path against the stars stays close to that of the Sun's. This is known as the ecliptic and it is often marked on star maps.

Jupiter is bigger and brighter than any star so it is not difficult to find. With binoculars you can see that, although it looks like a star, it is a round disk not a point of light. You should also be able to see four bright dots in a line on either side of the planet. These are Jupiter's largest moons, which were discovered by

Jupiter looks like a very bright star in the sky, and its four largest moons appear as small dots through binoculars.

METEOR SHOWERS

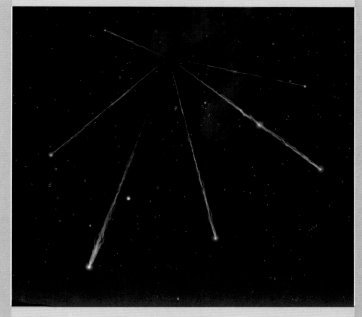

There is always a chance you might see a meteor, commonly called a shooting star, in the night sky. These are streaks of light made by pieces of space dust burning up as they hit the top of our atmosphere. At certain times of year there are meteor showers, when you can see many more shooting stars than usual. This happens when the Earth travels through a trail of dust left by a comet. The best time to see meteors is after midnight. They appear as a brief flash of light.

Saturn as seen through a large telescope. Its rings are sometimes tilted toward us, but at other times they are edge on and then they seem to disappear.

Galileo in 1610 through a telescope he built himself.

Saturn is disappointing when seen in the sky because you need a telescope to see its brilliant rings. Even with binoculars it just looks like a bright yellowish star. But if you see it through a good telescope, you will see one of the wonders of the Solar System. Saturn is the only planet whose rings are visible from Earth.

You can just see Uranus without binoculars, but not Nepture, although both are difficult to find even with binoculars – you have to know exactly where to look. For Pluto, you need a powerful telescope to see the smallest and most distant of the Sun's family.

SEEING SATELLITES

If you see a point of light moving steadily across the sky it may be an artificial satellite orbiting the Earth, or possibly a Space Shuttle or the space station Mir. These are sometimes seen in the evening sky after the Sun has set but while the satellite is still reflecting the Sun's light. They sometimes seem to flash on and off. This happens if they are spinning and thus reflecting the sunlight unevenly.

These are just a few of the fascinating sights to be seen. Try looking for them yourself and discover the many wonders of the night sky.

Comets which are bright enough to be seen in the sky without binoculars are rare.

117

8
DATA PAGES

THE PLANETS

	Mercury	Venus	Earth	Mars
Average distance from Sun in miles (million km)	36 (58)	67 (108)	93 (150)	142 (228)
Time to orbit Sun (year)	88 days	225 days	365.25 days	687 days
Time to spin once	58.6 days	243 days	23h 56m	24h 37m
Diameter at the equator in miles (km)	3,031 (4,878)	7,521 (12,104)	7,924(12,756)	4,217(6,786)
Number of moons	0	0	1	2

	Jupiter	Saturn	Uranus	Neptune	Pluto
Average distance from Sun in million miles (million km)	483 (778)	887 (1,427)	1,783 (2,870)	2,794 (4,497)	3,666 (5,913)
Time to orbit Sun (year)	11.9 years	29.5 years	84 years	164.8 years	248 years
Time to spin once	9h 50m	10h 39m	17h 14m	16h 3m	6d 9h
Diameter at equator in miles (km)	88,731 (142,796)	74,567 (120,000)	32,560 (51,800)	31,349 (48,500)	1,367 (2,200)
Number of moons	16	19	15	8	1

MOONS OF THE PLANETS

Planet	Moon	Discoverer	Year	Distance from planet in miles (km)	Diameter in miles (km)
Earth	Moon	-		238,861 (384,400)	2,160 (3,476)
Mars	Phobos	Hall	1877	5,829 (9,380)	14 (23)
	Deimos	Hall	1877	14,578 (23,460)	8 (13)
Jupiter	Metis	Voyager	1979	79,513 (127,960)	12 (20)
	Adrastea	Voyager	1979	80,147 (128,980)	25 (40)
	Amalthea	Barnard	1892	112,658 (181,300)	124 (200)
	Thebe	Voyager	1979	137,886 (221,900)	56 (90)
	Io	Galileo	1610	261,977 (421,600)	2,256 (3,630)
	Europa	Galileo	1610	416,889 (670,900)	1,950 (3,138)
	Ganymede	Galileo	1610	664,885 (1,070,000)	3,270 (5,262)
	Callisto	Galileo	1610	1,170,074 (1,883,000)	2,983 (4,800)
	Leda	Kowal	1974	6,893,680 (11,094,000)	9 (15)
	Himalia	Perrine	1904	7,133,536 (11,480,000)	112 (180)
	Lysithea	Nicholson	1938	7,282,669 (11,720,000)	25 (40)
	Elara	Perrine	1905	7,293,233 (11,737,000)	50 (80)
	Ananke	Nicholson	1951	13,173,429 (21,200,000)	19 (30)
	Carme	Nicholson	1938	14,043, 372 (22,600,000)	25 (40)
	Pasiphae	Melotte	1908	14,602,622 (23,500,000)	25 (40)
	Sinope	Nicholson	1914	14,726,899 (23,700,000)	25 (40)
Saturn	Unnamed	Voyager	1985	73,448 (118,200)	9? (15?)
	Pan	Voyager	1991	83,017 (133,600)	12 (20)
	Atlas	Voyager	1980	85,565 (137,700)	25 (40)
	Prometheus	Voyager	1980	86,622 (139,400)	50 (80)
	Pandora	Voyager	1980	88,050 (141,700)	62 (100)
	Janus	Dollfus	1966	94,078 (151,400)	118 (190)
	Epimetheus	Fountain Larson	1980	151,400 (94,078)	75 (120)
	Mimas	Herschel	1789	115,578 (186,000)	245 (394)
	Enceladus	Herschel	1789	147,890 (238,000)	312 (502)
	Tethys	Cassini	1684	183,310 (295,000)	651 (1,048)
	Telesto	Voyager	1980	183,310 (295,000)	16 (25)
	Calypso	Voyager	1980	183,310 (295,000)	16 (25)
	Dione	Cassini	1684	234,263 (377,000)	696 (1,120)
	Helene	Laques & Lecacheux	1980	234,263 (377,000)	19 (30)
	Rhea	Cassini	1672	327,472 (527,000)	951 (1,530)
	Titan	Huygens	1655	759,336 (1,222,000)	3,200 (5,150)
	Hyperion	Bond	1848	920,276 (1,481,000)	168 (270)
	Iapetus	Cassini	1671	2,212,763 (3,561,000)	892 (1,435)
	Phoebe	Pickering	1898	8,046,977 (12,950,000)	137 (220)

*Names in bold mean these are the larger moons.

Uranus	Cordelia	Voyager	1986	30,945 (49,800)	25? (40?)
	Ophelia	Voyager	1986	33,431 (53,800)	31? (50?)
	Bianca	Voyager	1986	36,786 (59,200)	31? (50?)
	Cressida	Voyager	1986	38,402 (61,800)	37? (60?)
	Desdemona	Voyager	1986	38,961 (62,700)	37? (60?)
	Juliet	Voyager	1986	40,017 (64,400)	48? (80?)
	Portia	Voyager	1986	41,073 (66,100)	48? (80?)
	Rosalind	Voyager	1986	43,435 (69,900)	37? (60?)
	Belinda	Voyager	1986	46,791 (75,300)	37? (60?)
	Puck	Voyager	1986	53,439 (86,000)	206 (170)
	Miranda	Kuiper	1948	80,470 (129,500)	293 (472)
	Ariel	Lassell	1851	118,685 (191,000)	721 (1,160)
	Umbriel	Lassell	1851	165,289 (266,000)	739 (1,190)
	Titania	Herschel	1787	270,925 (436,000)	1,000 (1,610)
	Oberon	Herschel	1787	362,269 (583,000)	963 (1,550)
Neptune	Naiad	Voyager	1989	29,827 (48,000)	31 (50)
	Thalassa	Voyager	1989	31,069 (50,000)	56 (90)
	Despina	Voyager	1989	32,936 (53,000)	93 (150)
	Galatea	Voyager	1989	38,526 (62,000)	93 (150)
	Larissa	Voyager	1989	45,982 (74,000)	124 (200)
	Proteus	Voyager	1989	73,324 (118,000)	249 (400)
	Triton	Lassell	1846	220,593 (355,000)	1,690 (2,720)
	Nereid	Kuiper	1949	3,261,551 (5,513,000)	211 (340)
Pluto	Charon	Christy	1978	12,241 (19,700)	746 (1,200)

Names in bold mean these are the larger moons.

CONSTELLATIONS

Constellation	English name or description	Constellation	English name or description
NORTHERN HEMISPHERE			
Andromeda	Legendary princess	Eridanus	River Eridanus
Aquila	Eagle	Fornax	Furnace
Auriga	Charioteer	Grus	Crane
Bootes	Herdsman	Horologium	Clock
Camelopardus	Giraffe	Hydra	Sea serpent
Canes Venatici	Hunting dogs	Hydrus	Water snake
Canis Major	Big dog	Indus	Indian
Canis Minor	Little dog	Lepus	Hare
Cassiopeia	Legendary queen	Lupus	Wolf
Cepheus	Legendary king	Mensa	Table (mountain)
Cetus	Sea monster (whale)	Microscopium	Microscope
Coma Berenices	Berenice's hair	Monoceros	Unicorn
Corona Borealis	Northern crown	Musca	Fly
Cygnus	Swan	Norma	Ruler
Delphinus	Dolphin	Octans	Octant
Draco	Dragon	Pavo	Peacock
Equuleus	Little horse	Phoenix	Phoenix
Hercules	Hercules, son of Zeus	Pictor	Easel
Lacerta	Lizard	Piscis Austrinus	Southern fish
Leo Minor	Little lion	Puppis	Ship's stern
Lynx	Lynx	Pyxis	Ship's compass
Lyra	Lyre or harp	Reticulum	Net
Ophiuchus	Serpent bearer	Sculptor	Sculptor
Orion	Orion the hunter	Scutum	Shield
Pegasus	Pegasus, the winged horse	Sextans	Sextant
Perseus	Legendary hero	Telescopium	Telescope
Sagitta	Arrow	Triangulum	Triangle
Serpens	Serpent	Triangulum Australe	Southern triangle
Ursa Major	Great bear	Tucana	Toucan
Ursa Minor	Little bear	Vela	Ship's sail
Vulpecula	Fox	Volans	Flying fish

Constellation	English name or description	Constellation	English name or description
SOUTHERN HEMISPHERE		**CENTRAL REGION (ZODIAC)**	
Antlia	Air pump	Aquarius	Water bearer
Apus	Bird of Paradise	Aries	Ram
Ara	Altar	Cancer	Crab
Caelum	Chisel	Capricornus	Sea goat
Carina	Ship's keel	Gemini	Twins
Centaurus	Centaur	Leo	Lion
Chamaeleon	Chameleon	Libra	Scales
Circinus	Compasses	Pisces	Fishes
Columba	Dove	Sagittarius	Archer
Corona Australis	Southern crown	Scorpius	Scorpion
Corvus	Crow	Taurus	Bull
Crater	Cup	Virgo	Virgin
Crux	Cross		
Dorado	Swordfish		

METEOR SHOWERS

Name of shower	Date each year	Average number of meteors per hour
Quadrantids	Jan 4	60 - 100
Lyrids	Apr 21	10
Eta Aquarids*	May 5-6	35
Delta Aquarids	July 29	20
Perseids	Aug 11-12	60 - 75
Orionids	Oct 22	25
Taurids	Nov 3-13	10
Leonids	Nov 17	10
Geminids	Dec 13	75

Difficult to see from Northern Hemisphere

The names indicate the constellations in the area of the sky from which the meteors appear to come, for example The Quadrantids, one of the most active showers of the year, seem to come from the constellation Bootes in the Northern sky. A meteor shower is usually spread over several days, but the dates given here are when you are likely to see most shooting stars (providing Moonlight does not get in the way).

TOTAL ECLIPSES OF THE SUN

Date	Time totality* lasts (minutes)	Where it can be seen
1994 Nov 3	4m 23s	South America
1995 Oct 24	2m 10s	South Asia
1997 March 9	2m 50s	Siberia, Arctic, Mongolia
1998 Feb 26	4m 9s	Central America, Carribean
1999 Aug 11	2m 23s	Europe inc. SW tip of England, Northern France, Germany, Switzerland, Austria, Southern Asia
2001 June 21	4m 56s	Southern Africa
2002 Dec 4	2m 4s	South Africa, Australia
2003 Nov 23	1m 57s	Antarctica
2005 April 8	0m 42s	South Pacific Ocean
2006 March 29	4m 7s	Africa, Asia Minor, Russia

This is a list of total eclipses, when the Sun is completely hidden. There are also partial eclipses, when only part of the Sun is hidden by the Moon. *Totality is when the Sun is completely hidden.

TOTAL ECLIPSES OF THE MOON

Date of eclipse	Time totality* lasts	Time of middle of eclipse (GMT*)
1996 Apr 4	1h 26m	00 11
1996 Sept 27	1h 10m	02 55
1997 Sept 16	1h 2m	18 47
2000 Jan 21	1h 16m	04 45
2000 July 16	1h 0m	13 57
2001 Jan 9	0h 30m	20 22
2003 May 16	0h 26m	03 41
2003 Nov 9	0h 11m	01 20
2004 May 4	0h 38m	20 32
2004 Oct 28	0h 40m	03 05

These are all total eclipses of the Moon, when the whole Moon is in the Earth's shadow. There are also partial eclipses, when only part of the Moon is in shadow. *Totality is when the whole of the Moon is in the Earth's shadow. *GMT = Greenwich Mean Time

SOME MILESTONES IN THE HISTORY OF ASTRONOMY AND SPACE

200 Ptolemy describes the Earth at the middle of the Universe with the Sun, Moon, and planets circling around it.

1054 Chinese astronomers see a supernova explosion where the Crab Nebula is seen today.

1543 Copernicus describes the Solar System with the Sun at the middle.

1609 Galileo starts exploring the sky with a telescope.

1668 Newton builds the first reflecting telescope.

1781 Herschel in England discovers Uranus, using a telescope he made himself.

1846 Neptune is discovered by Adams in England and Leverrier in France working independently.

1930 Pluto is discovered by Tombaugh in America.

1937 The first radio telescope is built.

1957 The first satellite, called Sputnik 1, orbits the Earth.

1959 Luna 3 space probe sends back the first pictures of the far side of the Moon.

1961 Yuri Gagarin becomes the first man to travel in space.

1962 The first successful space probe is sent to another planet — Mariner 2 flies past Venus.

1963 Valentina Tereshkova is the first woman in space.

1967 The first pulsar is discovered.

1969 Apollo astronauts, Armstrong and Aldrin, are the first people to set foot on the Moon.

1971 The first space station, called Salyut 1, is launched by the Soviet Union.

1972 The sixth and last visit of Apollo astronauts to the Moon.

1973 The US space station, Skylab, orbits the Earth and is home to three sets of astronauts.

1974 Mariner 10 spacecraft visits Mercury.

1975 Venera 9 sends back the first pictures from the surface of Venus.

1976 Two Viking spacecraft land on Mars, testing its soil and looking for life there.

1979 The two Voyager spacecraft fly past Jupiter.

1980-1 Voyager spacecraft reach Saturn.

1981 First Space Shuttle is launched.

1983 Pioneer 10 spacecraft leaves the Solar System, now beyond the furthest planet and traveling to the stars.

1986 – Halley's comet returns to be met by five space probes.
– Voyager 2 visits Uranus.
– Mir space station launched.

1987 Supernova explosion in the Large Magellanic Cloud is the nearest and brightest since 1604.

1987-8 Russian cosmonauts Titov and Manarov set the record for the longest stay in space of 365 days.

1989 – Voyager 2 arrives at Neptune, its last visit to a planet before leaving the Solar System.
– Galileo spacecraft is launched on its way to Jupiter. On the way it passes two asteroids, Gaspra in 1991 and Ida in 1993.
– Magellan spacecraft is launched to Venus, to orbit the planet and map its surface using radar.

1990 Hubble Space Telescope is put into orbit round the Earth.

1993 Space Shuttle goes on mission to service the Hubble Space Telescope.

1994 Pieces of the shattered comet Shoemaker-Levy 9 on collision course for Jupiter.

GLOSSARY

Asteroids Rocky chunks orbiting the Sun, mainly in a "belt," between Mars and Jupiter.

Atmosphere An envelope of gases around most planets, certain moons and stars.

Big Bang The name that astronomers give to the explosion which they think started the universe expanding.

Binary Star A pair of stars that orbit round each other, held together by the pull of gravity.

Black Hole A part of space where the pull of gravity is so strong that nothing, not even light, can escape. They may be created when a massive star collapses or may occupy the center of some galaxies.

Comet A small icy lump circling the Sun in a long, thin orbit. When it comes near the Sun, it develops one or more tails that always point away from the sun.

Constellation The patterns made by the stars in the sky. The whole sky is divided into 88 constellations.

Eclipse This happens when sunlight is blocked by the Earth or Moon. When the Full Moon goes through the Earth's shadow an eclipse of the Moon is seen. In an eclipse of the Sun, the Moon passes between the Earth and the Sun, blocking out sunlight for several minutes.

Galaxy A huge family of stars all held together by gravity.

The life of a star from new-born (left) to Sun-like star (center), then red giant (top) and finally white dwarf.

Gravity A force pulling any two things together. It holds the moons in orbit around their planets and the planets in their orbits round the Sun. Everything in the universe is affected by gravity.

Light Year The distance that light travels in space in one year, which is 5.88 million million miles (9.46 million million km).

Local Group of Galaxies The small cluster of at least 26 galaxies which contains our Galaxy.

Meteor (Shooting Star) The bright streak of light made by a small piece of dust or small rock burning up as it enters the Earth's atmosphere.

Meteor Shower Unusually large number of meteors, seen at regular times during the year, when the Earth goes through a trail of dust left by a comet.

Meteorite A larger rock from space that does not completely burn up in the atmosphere, and falls to the ground.

Milky Way The band of hazy light across the sky coming from faint stars in our own Galaxy, sometimes called the Milky Way Galaxy.

Moon A rocky body circling around a planet. Also the name of the Earth's only satellite.

Nebula A cloud of gas and dust in space.

Neutron Star A collapsed star that is very small and dense. It is made almost entirely of atomic particles termed neutrons. It spins rapidly (see Pulsars).

Orbit The path of one object around another in space, for example a planet moving around the Sun. It is the pull of gravity that keeps objects in orbit.

Phases The different shapes that the Moon seems to take as we see varying amounts of its sunlit side during its monthly orbit around the Earth. The planets Venus and Mercury also go through phases.

Planet A body circling around the Sun or another star. It shines by reflecting light from the Sun.

Pulsar An object giving out a series of regular pulses of radio waves, or sometimes light or x-rays. It is a neutron

An astronaut at work in space just outside the Space Shuttle.

star that spins round very quickly and sweeps a narrow beam across the sky.

Quasar A very bright object that is very far away giving out vast amounts of energy. Quasars are the most distant things astronomers can see in the universe.

Satellite An object in orbit around another larger object. Moons are called natural satellites, and man-made satellites and space stations are called artificial satellites.

Solar System The Sun and everything circling around it, including planets, moons, comets, and asteroids. It is held together by the pull of gravity.

Star A huge glowing ball of gas, making energy in its core and giving out heat and light.

Sun The central star of the Solar System. Compared with other stars it is average sized and middle aged.

Supernova A catastrophic explosion of a huge star at the end of its life.

Telescope An instrument that collects light, or radio waves, from distant objects.

Universe The whole of space and everything that exists within it.

Variable Star A star whose brightness changes over a period of time.

White Dwarf A small star that has collapsed when its hydrogen fuel has run out and it can no longer make energy in its core.

HOW TO PRONOUNCE WORDS IN THIS BOOK

Stress the part of the word printed in bold type to get the right sound.

Stars

Alcor	**al**-kor
Aldebaran	al-**deb**-ah-ran
Betelgeuse	**bee**-tell-gurz
Mizar	**my**-zar
Proxima Centauri	**prox**-im-ah sen-**tor**-ee
Rigel	**ry**-jel
Sirius	**si**-ree-us

Constellations

Andromeda	an-**dro**-me-da
Cassiopeia	kass-ee-oh-**pee**-ah
Centaurus	sen-**tor**-us
Orion	or-**ry**-on
Pegasus	**Peg**-as-us
Triangulum	try-**ang**-you-lum

Others

Deimos	**day**-im-oss
Magellanic	mag-el-**an**-ik
Mir	**meer**
Omega Centauri	**o**-meg-ah sen-**tor**-ee
Pleiades	**ply**-ad-eez
Phobos	**fo**-boss
Uranus	**you**-ran-us

INDEX *Numbers in italics refer to pictures*

PICTURE CREDITS

The Publishers would like to thank the following sources for their kind permission to reproduce the pictures used in this publication:

Anglo-Australian Telescope, with photography by David Malin; Armagh Planetarium; Julian Baum; Bridgeman Art Library: Giraudon/Musee de Torun, Torun, O'Shea Gallery, London, British Library, London, Royal Society, London; Caltech; Mary Evans Picture Library; Michael Freeman; The London Planetarium; NASA; Rex Features; Royal Observatory, Edinburgh; The Science Photo Library: Julian Baum, Sally Bensusen (1987), David Hardy, Peter Menzel, Ben Millon/Herman Heyn, Betty Millon, Gary Ladd, NOAO, David Nunuk, Mark Paternostro, Roger Rossmeyer, Royal Observatory, Edinburgh, John Sanford, Robin Scagell.

Thanks are also due to Andrew Simmen at The Science Photo Library.